# BUILDING A

# JOYFUL

# BUSINESS

*Stay Joyful!*
*Lianne*

## LIANNE KIM

Published in Canada, for Global Distribution
by YGTMama Media Co.
www.ygtmama.com/publishing
To order additional copies of this book:
publishing@ygtmama.com

Developmental Editing by Tania Jane Moraes-Vaz
Edited by Christine Stock
Cover & book design by Doris Chung
Author photo by Silvia Silva
ePub & Kindle Editions by Ellie Silpa

# READ THIS FIRST!

Hi friend,

Thank you so much for purchasing this book. To show you my gratitude, I want to gift you some joyful bonuses that include:

- The downloadable Companion Workbook for this book

- A secret BONUS chapter

These are complimentary resources that will help you get the most out of your reading experience.

TO DOWNLOAD, GO TO:
**www.liannekim.com/bonus**

Enjoy!

*Lianne*

To my mom and dad
who taught me to do what I love.

# TABLE OF CONTENTS

# INTRODUCTION

It was March 2013. From the outside, I had it all—a loving husband, Yoon, a beautiful baby girl, Julia, and another baby on the way. We lived in a bright and spacious apartment in a desirable midtown neighborhood, and I had a fairly lucrative sales job at an up-and-coming travel company at a hip downtown Toronto office. I was one of those women people looked at and said, "Wow, she really does have it all."

The truth is, I didn't feel that way on the inside.

My life was a hurried blur of obligations and appointments. Every day started out the same way: the never-ending hamster wheel of keeping up with . . . well, everyone. Each morning I'd rush through bathing and dressing myself and my kid, then we'd scarf down breakfast before I left for the office at 7:00 a.m., while my husband brought Julia to daycare. In the cold morning light, I would sit on the subway, dreading the day ahead and dreaming of a vastly different life.

I'd arrive at work, out of breath, by 8:00. There, I'd work on a mundane, purposeless list of tasks that lined the pockets of a wealthy, detached CEO. I was good at my job, but I wasn't lit up. I spent countless hours supposedly "on the clock," but in reality, I was planning my next vacation or aimlessly scrolling social media because, quite honestly, my job ceased to challenge me. In fact, I got through the bulk of my work by 10:00 a.m. on most days!

At precisely 5:01 p.m., I'd jump back onto a crowded, smelly subway so I could make it back to our apartment in time to drive to the daycare to pick up Julia. I would then rush home, all so I could hurriedly get dinner on the table, then rush through our meal, rush through bath time, and rush Julia off to bed. Yes, my husband helped a lot, and I am grateful for that help, but our evenings were anything but relaxing. In actuality, I didn't stop moving between 5:00 p.m. and 8:00 p.m. on most weekdays.

Once I put Julia to bed, I would breathe a sigh of relief that the "evening rush" was finally over. I could have a little "me time," which mainly consisted of collapsing on the couch in front of the TV. My exhaustion was compounded by the fact that we were expecting another baby in a matter of months. *How would I make room for someone else in all this panic?*

Although it might have seemed to others like I was living the dream, the reality was far from it. I was drained from leading a life lacking in meaning and contribution. I felt unfulfilled and uninspired, and I wasn't living at all—I was merely *existing*. But I wasn't put on this planet to merely exist.

For years leading up to this point, I longed to live a purposeful, passionate, and impact-driven life. I yearned to contribute in a meaningful way to society and let my true gifts shine through. As it stood, working in the corporate rat race for many years, I was utilizing about 1 percent of my skills and strengths, and for years that was okay . . . until it wasn't.

There was a voice in the back of my head, and at first it was just a whisper. "Psst! Lianne, you were meant to do more than this with your life." I tried my best to ignore this voice, but it kept coming back, louder and louder each time until it was so forceful that I simply couldn't ignore it anymore. The voice screamed, "YOU ARE WASTING YOUR POTENTIAL!"

I had always been a "good girl" who made "smart choices" and did what everyone expected of me. I did what others around me did—I played it safe. But I just couldn't do it anymore. I simply could not continue living like a spectator of my own life. It was time to stop depriving the world of my gifts and start living in a way that felt so much more, well . . . joyful.

From the earliest days of having an idea for my business, I knew JOY would play a big part. I didn't know much about starting or growing a consulting business, but I did know this fact: for self-employment to make sense for me, I had to approach it from the place of **having the life** I was dreaming about.

After all, working for someone else all those years had left me feeling hungry for change. I craved more freedom, more flexibility, more autonomy, and more respect from those I worked with. I dreamed of a life where I wasn't constantly rushing from place to place, trying to keep a million plates spinning in the air at once. I wanted to live a life where I could really savor the sweet moments it had to offer. Deep in my bones, I knew I wanted to be available for my kids alongside pursuing a mission-driven business. I wanted my kids to grow up knowing their mom was there for them while also making the world a better place, and I truly believed it was possible to do both. And doing both would require me to make some uncomfortable but important choices.

I'm lucky. I recognized early on in my life that I didn't want to spend the rest of it being miserable in a job I wasn't passionate about or, alternatively, eagerly waiting until I hit age sixty-five to retire and then "enjoying" whatever time was left. The truth is that most people don't realize their career is making them miserable until decades in. And what's worse? The moment they realize that *they* created it to be that way, that their life is a result of all the choices and the decisions they made or, conversely, didn't make. I didn't want to wake up one day only to find that I had become a servant to my own business. So, as I set out down this new path to build my own business, I knew that I needed to bake in the joy and the fun from day one.

As women, we learn to equate our self-worth with our ability to contribute in some way. For many of us, we feel worthy when that contribution is a financial one. And yet at the same time, we're told that it is equally important to maintain a clean house, raise well-behaved children, keep our partners satisfied, be present for our friends and families, etc. It is exhausting even thinking of the various roles and responsibilities we are expected to shoulder and execute every single day. And if we miss the mark somewhere, we may question our own self-worth.

**We are not conditioned to value our own personal fulfillment.**

So when those of us who set out to create a business do so, it is often with the aim of making a decent living. Replacing our income. Not going back to the corporate grind. The freedom to work on our own schedule, from the comfort of our homes or anywhere else we desire. And I believe those are good reasons. But a problem arises when we see financial gain as the only goal. And what I often witness in my now thousands of hours of coaching women is that we begin equating our self-worth with our income levels.

I set out to create a business that both fulfilled me personally and allowed me to enjoy life. I wanted to have it all, and that meant making very clear choices along the way—choices that a lot of my "mom boss" friends were *not* making.

For the first time in my adult life, I wanted to LOVE what I do. I wanted my days to feel fun and inspiring. I wanted to work with people I adored and help them live their best lives, all while having ample time for my marriage, my children, my friends, and myself. Sounds ludicrous, right? I mean who in their right mind would believe all that is possible? I'll tell you who . . . ME!

After spending several years coaching women and helping them create profitable businesses that light them up, I can tell you that the first step is to believe that it is possible for you. The next step is to design it that way. This book will help you do both these things.

### The real deal about this book

If you are looking for a book that shows you how to build a kick-ass business that dominates the market, crushes the competition, and allows you to rake in the dough at all costs, this isn't that book.

But if you are looking to immerse yourself in learning how you can build a business that allows you to showcase your true gifts and talents while embracing your own unique experiences and working with people you love (all while having the life of your dreams!), then, my friend, you have come to the right place. This is the book for you!

One of the values in my business is that *we bake in the fun from day one.* Success is not a destination you arrive at after years of hard work, struggle, and pain, nor is it a journey where you're finally allowed to celebrate your wins *only* once you get there.

HELL no! Celebration, fun, and joy need to be built into the foundation of your business and life. Joy should be infused into your business model as you go along. Fun and fulfillment should be key elements of the "what," "why," and "how" of your business. And that goes for everything—the people you serve, the team you build, the vision you are creating, the events you host, the services you provide, the way you spend your days, etc. It should permeate literally every aspect of your business.

Now that's not to say that every day must be blissful 24/7/365. That mindset is unrealistic, and frankly, it sounds exhausting to me.

But what if you could aim to spend 80 percent of your waking hours feeling fulfilled? Would that be cool? I sure think so, and I hope you do too. And in this book I'm going to give you the eight keys to making that happen. The journey all starts with getting clear on what you actually want to create and how you want to *feel* as you create your purposeful and passion-filled venture.

I recently polled my community of badass mamapreneurs. These women are not simply "self-employed"; they are rock-star entrepreneurs. They are movers and shakers, game-changers and thought leaders, change-makers and disruptors, and they are reaching incredible heights every damn day.

But this poll showed me another side of the story. It turns out that fewer than 35 percent of the women polled said they felt joyful in their businesses for 80 percent or more of their working time. (In truth, it is likely lower than 35 percent because it was a public poll. I suspect many of the women who don't love their work may feel embarrassed and therefore chose not to respond.)

My heart wants you to LOVE what you do at least 80 percent of the time, if not more. I know it is possible, but it is going to take some work.

Are you ready to start getting clear on what a joyful business looks like for you? We are going to have so much FUN together in these chapters, so buckle up, baby!

But first, be forewarned. Building a business based around JOY means going head-to-head with all the *it's not possible-ers*, the *dream-killers*, the *golden handcuffs*, and the *inner mean girl*. For example, the messages we receive from society, our loved ones, and industry leaders; the constant conditioning to play it safe, to cling to what's familiar, to cover up our unhappiness and continue masquerading ourselves in a world that tells us true happiness is a myth.

As you go on this journey with me, I ask you to do so with an open mind and heart. You need to be willing to question some of your societal conditioning and your own preconceived notions of what success is.

Another roadblock we all face is Other People's Agendas, or OPAs. Whether we care to admit it or not, we are hardwired for external approval. It is a basic human need to fit in and be liked. Often, when we start examining what we truly want for ourselves, we realize it is not in line with what other people would have for us.

People, including our parents, siblings, spouse, and closest friends, may have the best of intentions, but they can hold us back from becoming our greatest self with well-meaning yet simultaneously soul-crushing comments like "Are you sure it's a good idea to quit your job? There's no security in self-employment" or "How's that *little* business of yours doing?"

And in extreme cases, those very comments are enough to make some women quit pursuing their dreams and return to the safe, familiar box that has been carved out for them by society unless they decide to take a bold, unapologetic stand for themselves and do whatever it takes for each of them to make their visions come true.

This book will force you to question what you know about yourself, your potential, and your goals and dreams. It will challenge your notion of "success." Don't worry if some of your core beliefs get turned upside down as you read this book. They probably will. This book will make you acutely aware of some of the beliefs you currently hold that you think are protecting you but are actually holding you back from greatness.

*This book will make you straight-up uncomfortable.*

But on the other side of that discomfort lies freedom—freedom from what others think. Freedom from excuses. Freedom from all the crap currently keeping you small. Within the pages of this book are the keys to building a lasting, thriving business that not only lights you up but brings joy and value to others.

## Who this book is for

The book is written from the perspective of moi—a female business owner who just happens to be a mother. Therefore, the individual who will get the most out of this experience is likely a mom with a business or who plans to start one. It is for this reason that I have used the pronouns she/her and the nouns "women" and "female" throughout this book. With that said, even if you don't identify as such, if you find value within these pages, then this book is for you. Read on!

## Your Blueprint to a Joyful Business

From this moment forward, this book is your blueprint to a joyful business. Carry it with you wherever you go. Sleep with it if you have to. *I'm kidding . . . sorta.* This is the kind of book that will serve you today, tomorrow, and years from now if you take it seriously.

I have carefully curated a series of questions for each chapter. It's my hope that you treat this book like the resource that it is, and that you pause each time you see a question. Take the time to answer each one. Trust me, you'll be glad you did. It should take just a few minutes per chapter, and it can reveal wonders about you and the business and life you want to create.

**Note:** In order to make the most of this experience, I have compiled a number of downloadable tools for you at **liannekim.com/bonus**. So head over there and print them off so you can follow along with the exercises.

Consider this book a giant 50,000-word coaching session with one of the world's best business coaches (if I do say so myself). The questions I ask you to ponder are reflective of what it is like to be coached by me. These are the very same questions that have helped my clients reach six figures (and seven figures) for the first time, quit their day job, create a more balanced life, have better relationships, and grow their dream team.

Friend, let this be your blueprint. Follow the steps. Answer the questions. Do the work. I promise it will take you places you have only imagined.

### Are you ready? Let's play!

CHAPTER 1

# YOUR JOYFUL VISION

One of the hardest things I experience as a coach often occurs on the first day I start working with someone new. Our coaching typically begins with something I call a "Strategy Jam"—a full day where we sit down together and I help my client map out the vision they have for their own future. Their vision is usually murky and convoluted at first, yet just hours later, they leave that Strategy Jam with immense clarity on their goals and the strategy to achieve them.

It's a pretty epic day.

A powerful part of the day is an exercise called "Five-Year Vision" (let's call it 5YV for short). I ask my client to think about where they want to be five years from now. It's a simple question that often evokes a lot of heavy emotions.

I ask them to think about things like how they want to spend their time, who they want to serve, how much money they want to make, how they want to feel, what they want to accomplish. It's a lot to cover, and some women need a little more guidance than others, but they all get to a complete 5YV.

Here's the part that stinks. The majority of women have a really hard time with this exercise. They *umm* and *ahh* and squirm in their chairs. They go down a path and then stop and reverse. They share one powerful idea or thought but then quickly negate it. They second-guess themselves and their abilities. They fixate on thoughts of *But I don't know how I would do that* or *Maybe that's not the right goal.* They struggle with feelings of Imposter Syndrome and overwhelm . . .

They simply cannot dream big.

This pains me because it's a sign of what happens to us over time. *Want proof?* Think back to your own childhood. As kids, we believed that anything was possible. We explored trying on new roles. We allowed ourselves the freedom to experiment and saw ourselves in new and interesting ways. We were unfazed by what anyone said or thought. We weren't as guarded, and we sure as hell weren't apologetic about who we were. *Still don't believe me?* Take a look at your own child.

I see it in my daughter now. She's nine years old, and she loves trying new sports and activities. In fact, every time I suggest a new activity for my son to explore, if my daughter is within earshot, she'll pipe up, "I wanna try that!" even though I wasn't talking to her. She wants to do it all! She delights in playing "teacher" one day, "hotel critic" the next, and "Lego interior designer" the next. She's not concerned with *getting it right.* She's just enjoying the ride.

But over time, we lose this carefree approach to life—as we grow up and become a spouse, a mother, an employee, a homeowner. We gain responsibilities and duties. We prioritize everyone else's needs and goals and, in doing so, ours get pushed to the background. Like that favorite dress of yours that gets shoved to the back of the closet because "it's just not practical," our dreams start to fade away because, well, we let them. We downplay our desires, and it starts to feel like they don't even exist.

Think about it: **When was the last time someone asked *you* about *your* wildest dreams?** Unless you're working with a coach, it's likely that it was quite some time ago.

I want to change that.
Right now.
With this book.

I'm going to ask you some questions in the pages that follow, but before I do, I want to stress a few points here.

### First, there is no right or wrong.

When it comes to envisioning your version of success, there is one key thing to keep in mind: It's *your* version. It doesn't belong to anyone else. There is no right or wrong vision. Period. Really try to think about your own preferences and set aside anyone else's feelings. Notice when you're gravitating toward something that doesn't provide you with joy but *seems* like the right thing. If it comes with a feeling of "Well, I *should* want this . . ." or "I know I'm *supposed* to do . . . ," it's not the right vision.

Often, this feeling can come from a need for social status or external validation. For example, you might be saying to yourself, "All successful entrepreneurs have amazing cars!" But if you're satisfied with the car you have, who cares about all that noise? If your responses to these questions are coming from a place of comparison, then it's not your true, authentic vision, and it will never bring you joy.

For instance, we are a one-car family and always have been. We love our navy-blue VW Golf Wagon so much that we've even named it. We call it Blue Pajamas. It's efficient, reliable, and it only has 40,000 km on it! But recently, I felt pressure to drive something larger and more impressive. I thought it would make me *feel* and *look* more successful. After all, a lot of the famous entrepreneurs I look up to drive fancy SUVs by luxury brands, and I started to crave that status symbol too. Long story short, I caught myself and realized that I was falling prey to some pretty serious societal bullshit. So, we decided to hang on to trusty old Blue Pajamas for at least a few more years.

### Important: No skipping ahead!

In this book I've included several series of questions. You will get the most out of this experience if you answer the questions as you go, ideally writing them down in a notebook or on the downloadable PDFs from **liannekim.com/bonus**. I want you to do this work before skipping ahead. Within certain chapters, I've included a section on why I'm asking you that question. But if you understand my reason for including it, it might affect how you respond. So do yourself a favor and answer the questions before moving on. This practice will enable you to have the experience of being guided and coached rather than being directed toward the "right" response.

### Next, allow yourself to dream BIG!

In coaching, I often use the following prompts to help women let go of their constraints and really let loose with their dreaming:

- If anything were possible—the sky's the limit—what would you want?

- What would be a dream so big that if you achieved it, you'd blow your own mind?
- What would you do, what would you have, and who would you be if you knew you couldn't fail?
- What would the highest version of yourself be able to achieve?

So, despite some of our preconditioned habits to follow the rules, play it safe, and be "realistic" (I really hate that word), despite all that stuff, I want you to blow the roof off this thing with me. Besides, this book and this work is for YOU, and no one else. If you can't dream big within the quiet confines of these pages, you'll never be able to live those dreams out there in the real world.

**Finally, resist the need to know the how.**
As you do this work and get the big ideas out of your head and onto paper, somewhere along the way you'll be tempted to ask the dreaded question, "Ya, but how?"

But friend, trust me when I say this: **It is not your job to know the how, right now.**

Your job with these exercises is not to sabotage your progress by demanding to know the specific steps you'll take to make it happen. In fact, no one ever really knows the "how." Some of the biggest goals I have ever accomplished in business have come from a place of having no clue how I would get there. And whenever I reflect on how I did something, it's never exactly how I planned anyway!

**Dreaming doesn't require a plan, but planning does require a dream.**

Too often I see women who want to create plans and blueprints without getting clear on what the dream is first. It doesn't make sense. It's like getting in your car and asking the GPS for directions before you've put in the destination.

**Note:** I see this lack of rational planning a lot when business owners tell me they need a social media strategy, for example. But when I ask them what their business goals are, they don't know! It makes no sense! How can we create a strong strategy to attract customers to our business if we're not clear on what we want them to do when they get there?

Planning the route (the "how") without the destination (the dream) is absolutely nonsensical, and yet I see people trying to do it all the time. The trap is that when we feel busy, we feel productive. But here's something I want you to know:

*Busy does not equal happy, and don't fool yourself into thinking it does.*

When we start with a joyful dream that makes us excited to leap out of bed every morning, well, now we're onto something.

### Ready? Let's get dreaming!

I encourage you to get out a notepad and pen or jot down your answers on the downloadable PDFs. Do NOT skip ahead in this book before completing these questions.

## FIVE-YEAR VISION

Before we begin, I want you to imagine we are five years in the future. You are five years older, as are your spouse and kids, if you have them. You're living life five years from now. Complete this exercise from that place.

## Aaaand go!

- In five years' time, where will you be in life and in business?
- How will you be spending your days?
- What tasks are you focused on in your business?
- What do you do in your free time?
- You're serving only dream customers—who are they?
- How much money are you earning (your personal salary)?
- What does your team look like?
- What does your homelife look like?
- What does vacation time look like for you? Where are you traveling, and what does that experience feel like?
- What will you own that you don't currently own?
- How will you feel physically?

Now that you've completed this exercise, I want you to know why I asked you each of these questions. So, I'm including my reasoning here. Remember, no cheating. Do not read ahead until you've completed your answers.

Here are those questions one more time, and why they are helpful.

◎ **In five years' time, where will you be in life and in business?**

I ask this question because it's a nice open-ended one that allows my clients to take their dream in any direction they wish. It opens them up and gets them thinking and, hopefully, dreaming.

◎ **How will you be spending your days?**

As it turns out, most women live life in a "time-scarcity" mindset, meaning they feel like they never have enough time to do what they love. The truth is that most of us have ample time and we're just not prioritizing the things that bring us joy, be it business-related or personal. Getting clear on how we want to spend time during our waking hours helps shed light on both the business and life we want to create.

◎ **What tasks are you focused on in your business?**

This question helps women identify their "Zone of Genius," which I'll talk more about later on in this book. Most of us are working on things in our business that we don't find fun, things we're not very good at, or things that feel tedious/stressful/painful . . . the list goes on. Doing so hinders us from expressing our true gifts. Instead of shining boldly with our talents and creating the impact we desire, we stand in our own way, blocking our own success.

Getting crystal clear on our Zone of Genius and giving ourselves permission to focus on only those tasks that fall into that category can be incredibly liberating.

⊙ **What do you do in your free time?**

The sad reality is that for many women (especially those with kids), free time is nonexistent. They spend more than 75 percent of their time serving other people, and the other 25 percent of their time is spent asleep! The lack of free time is a problem, and something we need to fix. If you didn't have to work at all, what's something you'd gladly do all day? Got it? Great! Now you're on the right track!

⊙ **You're serving only dream customers—who are they?**

Far too many entrepreneurs settle for working with anyone and every-one who wants to pay them. This mindset is something we need to change. That's why I love the term "Dream Client," and I use it often in my work.

I believe we all deserve to work with Dream Clients all the time, but our thoughts and actions block us from that reality. Until we get crys-tal clear on the type of client we *really* want to work with, and believe we are deserving of their investment in us, we will continue to attract needy, low-vibe clients.

⊙ **How much money are you earning (your personal salary)?**

Historically, women do not demand to be paid what they're worth, and that's why we only earn a fraction of what men earn for the same work. This inequality is one of the reasons I am so passionate about helping women build their own businesses. It's one of the ways we can break through the glass ceilings and positively affect the statistics. When we control our own salary, we can create the same kind of wealth for ourselves in a way that may not be possible within more traditional workplaces.

You may be wondering why I ask you to think about "personal salary" and not "gross revenue." For most people, gross revenue can be hard to project, and it is not always directly linked to our own personal happiness. But what we pay ourselves—our personal salary—plays a much bigger role in our lives, especially if we are newer to business, which is why I start here. In other chapters we'll discuss gross revenue and the role it plays.

### ⊙ What does your team look like?

While customers are the lifeblood of your business, your team is the oxygen. Many women struggle with asking for help, but the truth is that we will get a lot further (and faster!) when we start to outsource things that are not within our Zone of Genius.

Your team are the people who surround you day in and day out. So, what does your dream team look like? Who are they? What qualities and strengths do they possess? How many people do you want to work with? Where and how will you work with them? How will you communicate with them? These are all important questions to think about.

**Fun Fact:** When my first business coach asked me this question, I blushed and shrunk in my chair. "Oh no," I swore up and down, "I don't see myself having a team. I just want to be successful on my own, doing what I'm best at. I don't want to manage people." How quickly those thoughts faded when I realized having a team was necessary to achieve the kind of joyful life and business (and impact) I envisioned for myself. I hired my first contractor about nine months into my business and never looked back.

⊙ **What does your homelife look like?**

Are you in your dream home now? This question is especially important if you work from home or plan to start doing so. Does your primary environment make you feel good and get you inspired and excited to be around it every day? If not, what does your dream space look like? What color is it painted? What kind of furnishings and accessories is it decorated with? If you have a home office, what is the energy of that space? Where do you want to be situated and what will it feel like when you're there? Is it a small town? Big city? Are you close to the mountains or water? Where do you see yourself when you think of your dream space or your forever space?

For many of us entrepreneurs, we spend a lot of our time in our primary residence, and many of us run our business from home. Our environment is absolutely a determinant of success and happiness. So, if you haven't thought about it in a while, now's your chance.

⊙ **What does vacation time look like for you? Where are you traveling, and what does that experience feel like?**

This topic typically comes up for most of the women I coach. They dream of taking more time off in interesting places with their loved ones, but they're putting it off for "someday," thus delaying the pleasure of these important experiences.

In fact, people who spend their money on quality experiences and making memories with loved ones often report having more feelings of happiness than those who spend their money on physical items. While buying that new outfit might bring instant gratification, it won't have the same lasting impact as spending the same amount of money on a spa day with your besties will. I want you to dream about how you want to live, and for many people, travel is a big part of that inspiration.

⊚ **What will you own that you don't currently own?**

Here's where I let people think about the toys they want to own, and the funny thing is, most of my women dream of pretty simple luxuries like a second vehicle to make life easier, or a laundry room on the main floor, or a stand-up desk. And guess what? There is absolutely nothing wrong with that. I don't care if you want a new pair of reading glasses or a tricked-out yacht . . . it's your dream. Own it!

⊚ **How will you feel physically?**

I ask this question because many adults are walking around feeling crappy most of the time. I wish it weren't the case, but it generally is. Thus, the trillion-dollar-and-counting health-and-wellness industry continues to grow every year.

But how we feel in our bodies is a major indicator of our overall happiness. After all, how many joyful, successful people do you know who complain of aches and pains all the time? Not too many, I assure you. When we feel good in our bodies, we can do more good in the world. When we do more good, we feel more fulfillment (AKA joy).

**Now that you've done that . . .**

Once you've completed this exercise, I encourage you to sit with your responses for a while. What emotions come up when you look at them? And is this really your dream?

It's not uncommon for powerful emotions to arise when I'm coaching someone. After all, we're talking about some major stuff here. It's not easy to do this work, and it's at this point in our session that many women start to tear up. I hear them say things like . . .

*"Why is it so hard for me to think big like this?"*
*"This dream isn't even that big. Why does it seem so impossible?"*
*"This makes me realize how small I've been playing."*
*"I know that to some people, this wouldn't make any sense."*
*"This seems so out of reach. How will I get here?"*
*"So much of what I used to want is not what I actually want."*
*"I'm not sure if this is what I'm supposed to want. Is this 'right?'"*

Dreaming big is challenging for us, especially as women, because it forces us to put our own wants and needs first, something we have not been conditioned to do for millennia. If we do this exercise right, it should evoke an emotional response. In fact, that's kinda the point.

And for many women, this exercise illustrates very painfully that the life they have lived for so long is not a reflection of who they long to be or how they want to live. Rather than pursuing their own dreams, they have become a servant to everyone else's.

Well, friend, that ends now, this very instant.

It's time we stop putting ourselves last on the list and start putting ourselves first!

Wherever you are in your life right now, as you read these words, there is only a finite number of years you have left on the planet. I want you to really think about this . . .

### How do you want to spend the remaining years on Earth?

Do you want to continue to do what your spouse/family/community expect of you? Do you want to continue to value what society deems as "worthy" of approval? Or are you prepared to create a life that is meaningful to *you*, joyful to *you*, successful to YOU?

If you already have a business, do you want to continue on the same path, doing the same work, in the same way, with the same people, feeling the same feelings from now until the end of time?

What I've asked you to think about in this chapter is to get super-duper clear on what success looks like for you, so you can chart a course for it. It's time to help you build your blueprint for a life that's true to you!

You might be wondering, *Can I revisit my answers, Lianne?*

Absolutely. But here's what I don't want. Don't revisit the exercise with the goal of watering down your wildest dreams in the name of making them more attainable. "Attainable" is highly overrated. I want you to strive for something slightly beyond your reach, even if you're not sure how you will get it.

Trust me, you'll figure it out as you go.

Growth happens when we are uncomfortable. And yet so many of us shrink away from opportunities for both personal and professional growth because of the looming pain we think will accompany it. We all know the old expression "no pain, no gain." We assume growth and progress only come as a result of grueling work and painful choices, but that simply is not true.

Just because something feels uncomfortable, doesn't mean it's impossible.

In fact, here's a list of things that I accomplished while feeling wildly uncomfortable:

- quit my first adult job to travel the world solo for a year
- ran a marathon
- got my black belt in karate
- moved across Canada to be with a boy (my now-husband)
- became a mother
- left an established sales career to pursue a business, with no guarantee of a paycheck
- hosted my first conference for mama entrepreneurs with absolutely no idea who would attend (MamaCon 2016)
- launched a podcast with no clue about what I was doing . . . at all
- grew a business with two children at home during a global pandemic
- wrote this book that you are reading right now

If I hadn't been willing to get a little uncomfortable, none of these amazing achievements would have happened.

*Hear me when I say this: If I can do it, you can too. So, let's make it happen.*

Real talk? There is nothing special about me. I'm not being self-deprecating. I'm being 100 percent genuine here when I say that I am not a unicorn. I was not born with any special powers. I did not go to business school. I did not get the top grades or have the highest IQ. In fact, in most regards, I'm pretty damn average.

So when I tell you that if I can do it then you can too, I'm not just blowing smoke up your ass. I really mean it. There's nothing I have that you don't, and nothing I have done that you can't—with a little effort.

The life of your dreams is out there, and you can have it. But it takes focus. It takes effort, consistency, and the willingness to start and the courage to keep going, no matter what. It takes grit, unshakable trust in yourself and your gifts, and a strong vision that you are relentlessly pursuing, no matter how uncomfortable it gets along the way.

So, are you ready to get a little uncomfortable with me? In the next chapter I'm going to help you define your "special sauce" and how you are meant to serve humanity. Big stuff, but you can handle it.

## FYI (For Your Inspiration):

I believe that every one of us deserves the right to draft our own dreams, not build someone else's vision of success. That said, sometimes a girl needs a little inspo!

Therefore, if you're curious, here's a glimpse of my current Five-Year Vision.

I wish to run a $25M company alongside a dozen or so amazing women of all walks of life. I dream of renovating our current home so that I have a kick-ass office and space to hold team and client meetings. I plan to work about twenty hours a week and to be done work every day by 3:00 p.m. so I can be available for my kids and cook delicious meals every night.

I want to travel four to six times a year to interesting locations—sometimes with my family, other times with just my husband, and other times on my own or with friends. I want to take my team on an incredible experience to help them achieve their own dreams and gain inspiration for their own work and lives. I see us learning and growing side by side in places like Brazil and Greece!

I aim to work out three to four times a week and maintain my current weight and fitness level. I see myself eating healthful foods prepared with love by me and the hubs and sitting down to eat as a family multiple evenings per week. I want to spend ten hours per week out in nature, breathing fresh air and being physically active (hiking, biking, swimming, etc.).

I plan to continue serving outstanding female entrepreneurs, helping them achieve their wildest goals and dreams. I want to have a strong, engaged social media following in the millions and to have thousands of women at our conferences each year. I wish for my podcast, *The Business of Thinking Big*, to have millions of downloads and to be consistently ranked as one of the best business podcasts in the world. I want to stand on stage with my business besties and mentors, joyfully coaching my women to greatness. I will have a published book (this one right here!) and probably one more.

I will have an incredible emotional connection to the most important people in my life (my husband, immediate family, and close friends), and I want to be able to treat those people to special experiences of a lifetime.

*Phew! How's that for a vision?!*

I'll be completely transparent with you. There was a time when declaring this vision would have been difficult for me. It would have felt terrifying and perhaps a little greedy. But I now have the clarity to know what's meaningful for me, and I do my best to avoid the pitfalls of societal norms and OPAs.

When I do this visioning work (which I sit down and do every few months), I can say with all certainty that **I want what I want because I want it, and I know in my bones it is possible**. It feels exhilarating to explore this vision in juicy, delicious detail and to share it with you here.

Clarity is a valuable first step in the process of designing the life and business of your dreams. Now that you have completed this chapter, you have a clear and compelling vision for your life as a whole. Congratulations!

But the Clarity Train doesn't stop there. Oh no! In fact, we are just getting started. Where we are headed next is even more fun.

In the next chapter we are going to look more specifically at your role and purpose within your organization—the "what" you do within your business.

# CHAPTER 2

# YOUR JOYFUL PURPOSE

When I first asked myself what I was put on this planet to do, I was overcome with massive waves of "I'm not ready to think about this yet." It seemed like such a big and important question, far too big for little ol' me to even attempt to explore.

You see, for the first half of my life I didn't think it was possible to love what you do. I mean I thought it was possible to do things you enjoyed, in the form of hobbies and interests, but the thought that anyone could make a decent living doing something they truly loved—and turn their passions into a source of income—well, *that* seemed downright insane. Too good to be true!

Until my big sister did it.

I was in my early twenties when my sister's life seemed to magically fall into place. She met the man of her dreams, they traveled the world together, and upon returning home, my sister opened her own photography studio. Shortly after, they got married, bought a house, and had a beautiful baby.

It seemed like the perfect life.

My life at the time was a far cry from that picture. I was fresh out of university and in my first sales job ever (which I sucked at). I was undervalued (and underpaid), single, and looking for love in all the wrong places. Despite my desire to be better at my job, I felt incapable of reaching out and asking for help, and the company seemed hell-bent on shoving me into a little tiny box, the "here's what you're good at, please do this and only this" box.

Oh, and did I mention I was making $24,000 a year?

Not only that, I was also certain this kind of annual salary was the norm, and that few people fresh out of postsecondary surpassed that figure. Boy, was I misled. My own friends and relations were making three and four times that amount their first year after graduating.

Ahhh, but I had chosen a career in *travel*, an industry that is known for grossly underpaying their staff and enticing young (naïve) people (mostly women) with the promise of exciting, exotic journeys. In short, I had convinced myself that because I had chosen a fun and sexy career path, I would be compensated not in the form of dollars in the bank but in "incredible life experiences."

As time went on, I didn't get any better at sales, and for various reasons, I felt more and more isolated from the others on my team. I had a low-paying job, no boyfriend, and a handful of friends, all of whom seemed to be leaps and bounds ahead of me. Additionally, I lived in a joyless apartment with three roommates who hated me.

*Could it get any worse?*

Well, yes, in fact, it could! At the same time I was floundering aimlessly, my smart, beautiful, and successful older sister seemed to be killing it at life. And now this?! *She's starting her own business? Who does she think she is?!*

And then the voices in my head started having a field day. I had a ton of opinions on the matter, none of which were remotely positive or factual. Here are some of the stories I was telling myself:

*"Well, of course she can start her own business—her boyfriend's footing the bill."*

*"Well, of course she can follow her dreams—our parents totally support her."*

*"Well, of course she can be successful—she has a better degree than I do."*

*"Well, of course she can take a risk—she has more savings than I do."*

Can you say *jealous much*? Even though I had no desire to start my own business at that time, or any specific skill set that I could parlay into a business, I still longed for what she had:

The ability to make a living on her terms, doing something she loved.

While I admired the hell out of her for having the courage to pursue her passions, I still saw her move as a rarity. *"Normal people don't just quit their jobs and start a business,"* I told myself.

Yep, pretty deluded.

So, while I was working a job I was not good at, alongside people I did not fit in with, and waitressing nights at the pub down the street just so I could pay the bills (did I not mention that part?), there was a part of me, way down deep, that craved something more.

I very timidly and with great trepidation started exploring the question, *If I could do something I loved, and make money doing it, what would that be?*

I started paying attention to some of the tasks, both at and outside of work, that truly utilized some of my greatest skills and gifts. You know, those things that you do so well and effortlessly that you would do them all day long even if you weren't being paid? Ya, those things. Some of those tasks included:

- setting up Lunch & Learns with guest experts for my office
- planning office events (if you're thinking about the Party Planning Committee from the television show *The Office*, you're not too far off)
- commuting to and from work on my bike—often my favorite part of the day
- having a blast with my waitressing customers at the bar (I really did have a way with the fellas back then, and let's face it, the tips were hard to beat)
- putting together talks/presentations and delivering them
- mentoring the younger women I worked with on things like finances (I was such a master, since I was making $24,000 a year. But I still knew more than the girl making $23,000 a year.)
- arranging theme nights and group outings for my friends
- writing descriptions of our programs for our marketing materials and training docs
- listening and giving (unsolicited) advice to my friends in need *(Hello, did someone ask for a coach?)*

You see, even though I felt as if I didn't have what it took to start my own venture and generate my own money (that part downright terrified me), I was starting to become aware of things that I did well that also brought me joy.

In fact, if you look again at that list, you'll see a striking resemblance to my current job description as CEO of my own company, which looks like this:

- hiring, training, and leading my own team
- planning networking events and conferences for our customers
- doing morning workouts and midday #CEOtime walks
- designing and delivering webinars and video trainings
- mentoring, teaching, and coaching my clients and students
- hosting fun social gatherings with my mastermind women including my annual client-success celebration and women's retreat
- creating content (podcasts, programs, this book, etc.) that help spread my vision
- listening and giving advice to people who pay me to help them move forward

What I am attempting to illustrate with this comparison is that often the things that we gravitate to and enjoy when we are younger are the very same things we were put on this planet to do.

I wholeheartedly believe—no, I KNOW—in my heart of hearts that I am here on Earth to help women grow, succeed, and live their wildest dreams. I do that through my free content (my podcasts and trainings), my paid programs, and, you guessed it . . . this book. That is my purpose for being, and I'm living it every damn day. Yeehaw!

But that last part is new. I didn't give myself permission to live my purpose until the ripe old age of forty. Why the hell not, you ask? Well, here's a list of things that stopped me from owning and expressing this vision:

- fear of what my parents might say
- fear of what my friends might say
- fear of what people at my job might say
- fear of what my boyfriend (now husband) might say

Are you sensing the theme here? Well, if not, don't worry, you're in good company because for many years I was totally aloof to the fact that FEAR of what other people thought of me was holding me back from living a life of purpose and meaning.

Instead, I toiled away for more than fifteen years building someone else's dreams. Until I couldn't anymore.

### How I made the leap

Have you ever had one of those weeks where you happened to hear a random word or name not just once, or twice, but THREE times and then you think to yourself, *Hmm, maybe this is some sort of sign.*

It was a few weeks before my fortieth birthday when I had one of those weeks. Three different people in three different scenarios all mentioned the same random name: Tony Robbins.

I didn't know much about Tony except that he had a series of programs designed to help people be their best selves, or something like that. Honestly, it all seemed a bit bogus to me. But given that I was about to turn forty and had heard his name three times in one week, I chose to see this as a sign and go online to see what ol' Tony was up to.

A lot, as it turned out.

His website had a robust list of events, programs, and courses one could take with him to better their life and basically become an awesome human being. I didn't particularly feel as if my life needed bettering, but something drew me to click on his "Upcoming Events" tab, and there I saw his three-day retreat called *Unleash the Power Within*.

It happened to be taking place in Dallas, Texas . . . in three weeks.

Again, let me be clear. I didn't seek out this opportunity, but it seemed to be calling to me. *What would I learn if I went there? Could I even get there? Could I get time off?* And, of course, the dreaded *What would Yoon say about all this?* The wheels were turning.

This was bonkers. I hadn't planned to go to an event in Dallas in three weeks. *Don't most people sign up for this stuff like months in advance? Don't people plan for this stuff? Budget for it?* I most certainly had no plan or budget.

And yet, I couldn't stop thinking about it.

I decided to let the fates decide. So rather than muscling or forcing it, I simply said, *"If this is meant to be, the universe will make it so."*

I started looking into what I would need to make the trip happen.

*Could I get transportation?* Turns out I had more than enough points to fly for free. I just had to pay the nominal taxes. Score!

*Could I get accommodation?* As luck would have it, I was able to use my travel agent discount at a well-known luxury hotel chain to secure a room for $69 a night. Yes, you read that correctly (now you see why people go into the travel industry).

*Could I get time off?* A quick email to my boss determined that it was indeed possible to secure the time off.

*Could I get a discount on the conference ticket?* This discount was not a requirement for me, but I was curious to see if the stars were really aligning to make this happen. And yes, they were. The sales agent replied that she'd be happy to offer me a $100 discount on the event ticket, making the entire four-night trip to Dallas from Toronto less than $1,000 including flight, accommodation, and access to the event!

Well, now that it appeared the universe did have a plan for me, the time had come to talk to Yoon about it.

I love my husband, but he and I are *very* different people. I am a dreamer. I am a little wild and unpredictable. I am spiritual. I am an early riser. I prefer vegetables to meat.

He is none of those things. Polar opposites might be an understatement when describing us.

And at the time of this event, I really worried about what he would think or say in response to the fact that on my fortieth birthday, I wanted to flee the country and leave him and our two toddlers behind to go and spend four days with a public figure who might as well be the Bono of the personal development world.

I broached the subject with much trepidation, and I even stumbled over my own words as I set him up for the bomb I was about to drop on him. He smiled at me and simply asked, "You're not joining a cult, are you?"

I laughed and then explained what I had in mind and how it was something I just felt called to do, that I wasn't sure exactly why, or why now, but it seemed like something I was meant to experience.

He supported my decision and even helped me book the flights. I set off on my way to Dallas, and when I came back, I had gained the clarity I was looking for:

I had a plan to quit my job and start my own business.

**Life Lesson:** Sometimes the universe knows exactly what you need, even if you don't!

I had a good fifteen years under my belt of working in various corporate environments, usually at a desk, usually doing some form of sales. I'd already started Mamas & Co., which, at that time, was just a little local moms' meetup group. I had begun exploring helping some of the mamas with their sales and marketing plans, and I LOVED it.

I remember one night when about seventeen mamas, all with different businesses at different ages and stages, gathered at my home in Toronto.

Our little group was just a few months old, and I had been noticing some of the women were struggling with issues of self-confidence, something that was affecting their sales. I could totally relate. (You'll recall my first sales job was not a smashing success.) When I told them I had a few tips and tricks that I thought could help them grow their businesses, they were more than excited to come to my home to hear my ideas.

Keep in mind that these were new moms, many of them with kids under the age of three. Looking back, I think they were just thrilled for a night out and a glass of wine. One woman who had a newborn at home was so exhausted that she literally kept nodding off the entire two hours I was speaking!

And yes, I spoke for *two whole hours!* Let's just say that on that night I had little understanding of building a powerful, transformative presentation that left them wanting more. Rather, I droned on and on about the foundational concepts of sales and gave them several techniques that would help them articulate their own value and generate more revenue. Nothing I shared was earth-shattering news. In fact, much of it was old hat to me by then.

But there was a moment. About halfway through the presentation, I hit my stride and was sharing some concept that was particularly evocative. I looked out into the audience of women sitting in my living room, and I felt that several of them were completely enthralled by what I was saying. They were leaning in, nodding, smiling . . . I knew what I was sharing was really resonating with them.

**In that moment, I felt what it was like to change someone's life.**

And I wanted more.

After Dallas, I sat down with my husband and declared, "I will not be at this job come 2017." That was July 2016, and that declaration became fact. Later that fall, I walked into my boss's office and announced I was leaving to start my own business. My official last day at that company was December 31, 2016.

Why am I sharing this story with you?

I want you to see that if you're struggling to identify exactly what you were meant to do in this life, I don't blame you. Again, it's not your fault at all. Society is set up this way. If you're finding it near impossible to do meaningful work that people appreciate and reward, I get it! If you haven't quite uncovered your own unique skills and strengths, fear not, this chapter will help.

I have been where you are, and I know there is a way out. And I want to show you that in this book.

You've already done one of the hardest parts of this journey: defining your vision for your life. If you completed that exercise in Chapter 1, you've done something that likely 90 percent of the population hasn't done—created time and space to **dream big**.

In this chapter I want to help you identify precisely *how* you will build a business so that you can live that dream life. But we're not building just any business! We're building a business around your "special sauce," those indescribable, 100 percent unique and remarkable talents that no one else possesses quite like you do.

Don't believe it's possible? Here are some of the women I have helped achieve amazing things in this area:

### Meet Liat

When I first started working with Liat, she had left her corporate career after thirteen years to pursue her passions. She had a dream of becoming a transformative life coach, and yet she didn't have a single client. Within six months, we got clear on who she was meant to serve and the kinds of transformations she could assist these women with. We designed and priced her first coaching package. We also developed and implemented a system for attracting and converting leads. She set to work, and the customers started to come. At the beginning of our work, Liat set a goal of having a roster of ten powerhouse clients, and by our final week of working together, she achieved exactly that.

### Meet Tammatha

When Tammatha and I first met, she had just experienced a season of profound grief after losing both her mother and her stepson in a matter of weeks of one another. She had a growing accounting firm and was wearing all the hats in the business. She had a team that was underperforming, and as a result, she was bearing the brunt of the load. Tammatha put a plan into motion to have only the right people on her team and to empower them with the tools they needed to succeed. She went from working sixty-hour weeks to just twenty-five-hour weeks and crossed into the seven-figure arena, all while having more than enough time for her husband, kids, and her true passion, golf!

**Meet Nathalie**

Nathalie is an incredibly talented photographer who decided to build her business on the side of a demanding day job. Despite her plans to leave that job, her employer kept tempting her to stay by offering her more recognition and a higher salary. Nathalie was burning the candle at both ends, fitting in photography on weekends and days off. Soon, she grew overwhelmed and started feeling disconnected from her partner and kids because she was always working. Nathalie knew something had to give, so she mapped out the exit strategy for her day job. Within a matter of months, she made the leap to self-employment, and within a year of that, she hit six figures in her business.

Although their stories are unique, each of these women has one thing in common. They came to me with the idea of a dream business they wanted to create. They all wanted a better life for themselves, and that required them to focus on specific areas.

And within months, I helped each one of them turn their idea into a thriving business, serving their Dream Clients and doing only those things they were born to do.

Now it's time for me to help you.

You'll want to grab a notepad and pen or fill in the downloadable PDFs at **liannekim.com/bonus**. Remember, no cheating! Don't skip past this part or you'll be robbing yourself of the critical clarity you need to build a joyful business.

- **What did you love to do as a kid? What job did you fantasize about having one day? What roles did you assign yourself when you played make-believe?**
- **In what roles have you stepped up as leader, teacher, or mentor? What are the subjects you love to educate others about?**
- **What are the things you would do all day long, even if you aren't being paid?**
- **What do people say you do better than anyone else?**
- **What are you most proud of accomplishing in the last five years?**
- **Where do you feel you really shine? When you take center stage and all eyes are on you, what are you doing?**
- **What activities in your work give you that feeling of "I'm reaching my highest potential"?**

Once again, I really hope you're not skipping over the above work. I must stress the importance of it. This work is what is going to get you living your best damn life. Got it? Good.

Now, once you've completed the above questions, feel free to read on to learn why I included them.

- **What did you love to do as a kid? What job did you fantasize about having one day? What roles did you assign yourself when you played make-believe?**

When we're kids, we have no limits. Our parents and teachers encourage us to "reach for the sky" and assure us we can do "anything we set our mind to." Yet somehow, as we continue to grow older, things shift, and we stop believing anything is possible. But we, as human beings, what makes us us, doesn't actually change that much as we age.

For example, I still enjoy a lot of the things I enjoyed as a kid, such as teaching others (I was always the teacher when we played school), performing (I was constantly singing, dancing, telling jokes around the dinner table, and putting on plays), and developing artistic projects (I'd get an idea, then just had to go create it).

When we're young, we let our authentic gifts shine every single day, but as we age, we swap those gifts for more practical roles that we feel we must do as it's "all a part of growing up." We trade in what's fun for what's logical, and our lives reflect that. We end up in jobs or businesses we can't stand, grinding it out, living for our weekends and our three weeks of vacation a year.

But it doesn't have to be this way. That's why I ask you to think about what you loved when you were young. If you had the time, money, and freedom, would you do that now? Or some version of that? Of course you would. My husband loved to skateboard as a kid, and what does he do when he has time off now? He goes on phenomenal snowboarding trips all over the world with his buddies. This past year he met his friends in Japan for two weeks of some of the best slopes and sushi he's ever experienced.

Spend some time exploring the past and you will absolutely design a better future.

⊚ **In what roles have you stepped up as leader, teacher, or mentor? What are the subjects you love to educate others about?**

Typically, the things we gravitate to are the things we're good at. Often, the things people turn to us for advice and guidance on are the things we know so well that we don't even realize it is a gift. We take it for granted.

So, what do people turn to you as the expert in? Where do you find you're constantly teaching or leading others? There's likely a reason. Follow that trail and see where it leads you.

⊚ **What are the things you would do all day long, even if you aren't being paid?**

In my coaching work, I talk a lot about helping people find their "flow state." What is flow, you ask? To me, flow is defined as being in a state of high-quality output. You might call it "being in the zone."

You're doing work that you love so much, that comes to you so fluidly and effortlessly that you could do it all day long. It literally doesn't feel like work. Time seems to pass rapidly, and you look up to see you've been "working" for the last four hours. It feels like play. And that's the point!

As I am writing these words, I am finding myself in a state of flow. I sat down to write this book today, and I am already several pages in. I have typed nonstop for the last seventy minutes, and it is the *second* time today this has happened. That is how I know I'm working in my Zone of Genius. I'm writing, and it feels like fun and not at all like work. Therefore, I know *this* is the book I was meant to write (after three attempts at writing a book in the past few years).

I have found my flow, and thus, I'm in the right place.

⊚ **What do people say you do better than anyone else?**

It can sometimes be difficult to accurately assess our own strengths, and we are often our own worst critic. That's why it can be helpful to get feedback from others.

Think of your friends, colleagues, peers, partners, and clients. What do they love about you? Not sure? Go back and look at past texts, emails, and social media posts. If you have a business, go look at previous reviews and testimonials. If you're struggling to identify what's awesome about you, don't worry. There is always someone out there willing to do the job for us.

⊚ **What are you most proud of accomplishing in the last five years?**

While I don't think *achievement* is the ultimate marker of a life well lived, I do think it's helpful to identify what tasks give us that sense of accomplishment and why. Are you proud of helping a friend through a messy divorce? Perhaps a career as a coach is in your future. Feeling jazzed about that big account you landed? Perhaps sales is the thing that most excites you. These are all signs that may help us identify what we deem as meaningful contributions.

⊙ **Where do you feel you really shine? When you take center stage and all eyes are on you, what are you doing?**

A lot of my clients are self-proclaimed introverts who avoid the spotlight. However, when we are good at what we do, the spotlight finds *us*. One area I have shined in throughout my life is public speaking. Without any special training or attention, I often won speech contests in school and was valedictorian at my junior high graduation. I never actively thought, *Gee, I'm good at this,* but it seemed the chance to shine almost *sought me out.*

As I grew older, I recognized and fostered this gift. I started to seek out opportunities where I could lead through speaking and eventually built a thriving business around my ability to move an audience through my words. So, think about this: rather than where are you seeking the spotlight, ask yourself **where is the spotlight finding me?**

⊙ **What activities in your work give you that feeling of "I'm reaching my highest potential?"**

Now, if you are stuck in a mediocre job that you hate, moments of living your highest potential may be few and far between, so I ask that you really think about this one. Are there moments in your day, week, or even year when you can look back and say, *"Yes, that was me at my absolute best"*?

If so, what are those moments? Really take a minute to revel in that memory, and relive it for a few seconds with me now. What did it feel like to see your top gifts shining through for all the world to marvel at? How did you feel? What was it that allowed you to experience your own full potential?

It is important we thoroughly understand these elements in order to chart a course for greatness, so if you merely skimmed the last few pages, stop reading now. Grab a pen. Go back and don't stop until you've responded to all the questions so far in this book.

After all, how can we build a life and a business of our dreams if we don't get clear on how we are meant to serve others?

I'll admit some of the questions may seem a little out of left field, and I am not suggesting that just because you liked animals as a kid that you become a dolphin trainer or start a dog-walking business. But I am suggesting that you can use the answers to these questions as clues to where your true passions lie. Don't look at the actual words on the paper, **look for patterns and trends**. What are you noticing as the subjects and roles you tend to gravitate toward? And conversely, what do you see as areas that are not your strengths?

*Lianne, are you asking me to identify my weaknesses?*

Yup, I sure am! And yes, I know it can be a challenge to own your weaknesses, but I promise you, knowing your strengths and weaknesses is a gift!

There can be immense value in clarifying not only where you should be spending more time but also those areas that you are just not meant to further develop. Labeling those tasks that do not light us up, that we're not strong in, can provide powerful clues into our own purposeful path.

For example, once upon a time I was in a business partnership. My partner and I shared the load of running a thriving community, and we worked well together. But I often felt guilty about shying away from certain analytical or detail-oriented tasks . . . that is until I read the book *Rocket Fuel* by Gino Wickman. In it he describes the difference between a Visionary (all the things I naturally gravitate toward) and an Integrator (all the things I avoid like the plague).

It wasn't until I read that book that I realized there is nothing wrong with being bad at stuff. Rather than feeling guilty for not being more organized, thorough, and precise, I began to celebrate and seek out opportunities that allowed me to express my true gifts of visioning, creating, and inspiring others.

For years I felt ashamed about not being better at so many things. Wickman's book freed me from those feelings and helped me see myself for who I truly am—a Visionary! I now lead a team of people, each with their own unique gifts that we leverage in my business. My role is to develop and grow the vision, and their roles are . . . everything else.

So, take a few moments to answer these all-important questions.

- **What tasks do you find frustrating, hard, or draining?**
- **What tasks seem to take longer than they should?**
- **What are some of the things you spend time doing (merely because you know you "should") but you'd rather be doing anything else?**

- What tasks tend to remain on your weekly to-do list, week after week after week, and never seem to get crossed off?
- What tasks do you feel are an utter waste of your time and talents?
- What tasks do you wish you could just pay someone to do for you to get them off your plate ASAP?
- What tasks do you feel are keeping you from doing more of what lights you up? What tasks get in the way of you reaching your highest potential?

Once again, after you've put pen to paper, I'll share my reasons for including these specific questions.

- **What tasks do you find frustrating, hard, or draining?**

In essence, what do you suck at doing? Remember, there's no guilt or shame here. This is merely an opportunity for you to identify those areas that may be slowing you down or creating bottlenecks in your business.

For me, these tasks include:
- writing detailed copy (I'm much more of a talker)
- analyzing financial statements (that's why God invented book-keepers! Thank heavens!)
- setting up tech stuff (that's why God invented integrators!)
- doing video or audio editing (that's why God invented editors!)

Are you sensing a theme here? There are trained professionals whose passion it is to run a Profit and Loss statement, build a slide deck, edit a podcast . . . and those people LOVE to do those things. But those people are not me. If you find a task too difficult or draining, own it, then let it go. Someone else will gladly do it.

⊚ **What tasks seem to take longer than they should?**

When we're slow, we're not in flow. Flow state moves quickly. It's energizing and exciting and often feels a bit frantic. But if you're moving at a snail's pace, that's often a sign that some part of the task is bogging you down. Maybe it's time to outsource that bad boy.

⊚ **What are some of the things you spend time doing (merely because you know you "should") but you'd rather be doing anything else?**

Looking back on my first year in business, this task was most definitely my blog. I knew it was important to publish a weekly blog, and while I enjoyed the creative aspects of it, I dreaded other stuff, such as editing and uploading it to my website and optimizing it for SEO purposes.

I felt like I *should* be doing all blog-related tasks, but I honestly had no desire to do them.

As I'll share later, I found someone who delighted in the parts that I found agonizing, and after a short trial run, I hired her and never looked back.

⊚ **What tasks tend to remain on your weekly to-do list, week after week after week, and never seem to get crossed off?**

This question is an easy one. Just review your to-do list from the last several weeks and check for what is not crossed off. Again, look for patterns and trends. Essentially, we are looking for those tasks you avoid in favor of more enjoyable, flow-state tasks.

Somehow, I always manage to record my podcast, but updating my billing information for a certain software just never gets crossed off that list. And that's okay. Knowing what we shy away from helps us identify where we should *not* be spending our time and energy. And having this information is a very good thing!

- **What tasks do you feel are an utter waste of your time and talents?**

I hate to be that girl who thinks that she is above certain tasks, but I can tell you this: I haven't spent the last twenty-plus years in sales, marketing, and leadership so I can clean the toilets. It may be someone's dream job, but it isn't mine.

- **What tasks do you wish you could just pay someone to do for you to get them off your plate ASAP?**

Here's the best part of this question: once you've answered it, you get to go out and do exactly that: pay someone! I've hired out everything from cleaning my house to mowing the lawn to doing my taxes to creating my social media posts . . . you name it, there's someone who's making money doing it. By giving this work to them, you are letting them live their wildest dreams of earning money on their own terms. Win-win!

(If letting go of a task feels scary right now, don't sweat it. I've dedicated an entire chapter later in this book to your team. Stay tuned.)

- ◉ **What tasks do you feel are keeping you from doing more of what lights you up? What tasks get in the way of you reaching your highest potential?**

These are often tasks that need to get done, but they feel cumbersome—the "buzzkill" of all your duties. Not sure what I'm talking about? Just look at next week's to-do list.

If you were to only focus on items that helped you fully live your mission, what wouldn't make the cut? I bet you already know, but you might be clinging to those tasks for some reason or another. So, get clear on these soul-suckers and then let them go. You'll likely feel an instant sense of relief, which is a sign we're on the right track.

Okay, friend. We did some great work in this chapter. High five!

Now that you've uncovered the life you were meant to live and how you were meant to serve others, it's time to start building a business around those things.

**You ready? Let's go!**

CHAPTER 3

# YOUR JOYFUL CUSTOMERS

*Who* we spend our time with is a big indicator of how much joy we will experience. For many of us, the people we spend the most time with in our businesses are our clients. Our clients are amazing, wonderful human beings who, in most cases, trust us long before anyone else does and pay us actual money to do the things we love.

When you think about it, clients are pretty freakin' awesome.

But what about when they are *not* awesome? Can we talk about that for a sec? Because this reality is something I see that hinders a lot of people from having the business of their dreams. They love what they do, they do it well, they are making a name for themselves (and yes, getting paid), but they're attracting total duds.

Why is this happening?

Let me take a few moments to describe a pattern I have seen all too often.

### Meet Joanne

Joanne is a mom of two kids, and she decides to quit her corporate job to start her own business. She's taking a big leap, and she's excited, but also scared. She really needs to make this work. In the early days she enjoys what she does, and she's ecstatic that anyone wants to hire her. She doesn't really care who hires her, she's just grateful to be doing what she loves and to be getting paid. So, she attracts a wide variety of people, all with different needs. She does her best to serve them all, even though some are not exactly a perfect fit.

Some customers don't want her existing offers and some don't agree with her pricing, so she "customizes" a package just for them. After all, if she doesn't make them happy, they'll go to someone who will. She doesn't want to be too picky.

It's thrilling to be making a go of her business, but after a while, things start to get messy.

Over time, Joanne's clients start mistreating her. They don't respect her boundaries because she doesn't have any. They walk all over her, asking for more of her precious time and energy. Because Joanne feels like she has to take the work (because if not, who knows when the next client will come along?), she keeps her head down and her mouth shut. She delivers on her clients' every request, even though it's beyond the scope of what they've hired her to do. She's at their beck and call because she believes it's important to go *above and beyond*, especially in the early days when you're trying to prove your worth.

Before long, Joanne's personal life is nonexistent, and she's working around the clock. Her family is frustrated by her lack of presence. She gets emails, calls, and texts from her clients at all hours, demanding this and that, and she always responds right away, even if it's during dinner or her daughter's birthday party.

Joanne grows frustrated, but she's not sure what she can do. If she changes things now, how will her clients react? They've come to expect a certain level of "service" from her, and she doesn't want to lose them.

On and on Joanne goes down this path until . . . she burns out. She's simply had too much of it. She starts dreading getting out of bed in the morning for fear that when she does sit down to work, it will be an endless stream of requests to respond to and fires to put out. She no longer feels the same love she once did for her business and is considering getting a day job.

Joanne hasn't built a joyful dream business. She's built a *nightmare*. And all because she didn't take time to get clear on the type of client she wants to serve.

My hope is that this scenario doesn't apply to you, but perhaps some aspects of Joanne's story sound familiar. And if they do, don't despair, friend. This scenario is quite common among female entrepreneurs, especially in the early years.

Here are some of the most common missteps I see when it comes to who we serve:

- We're not clear on the kind of client we want to serve, and it shows. Our marketing and messaging are all over the place as a result.

- We're scared to niche down for fear we'll leave someone out or lose sales.
- We don't set clear and consistent boundaries with our clients from the start, and if we do, we don't uphold those boundaries when it counts.
- We don't clearly communicate our policies and procedures with our customers (often because we don't have any).
- We let our clients call the shots in the name of "customer service" when really, we're being ruled by our fear of people not liking us.
- We resist speaking up when a client behaves poorly.
- We hang on to a client for far too long, well after things have gone sour.

I don't want you to experience any of these situations (or the fallout that comes with them). That's why I've included this chapter, to help you get clear on who you really want to serve. Take a moment to answer these questions about your Dream Client.

**Important:** As you do this exercise, I don't want you thinking of *just anyone*. In fact, the more you focus on the *exact person* you want to serve, the better. Think about the kind of person you want to serve in your business, someone who is topnotch in your eyes. Not an average client but your true Dream Client (I'll call them DC for short), someone you'd be over-the-moon ecstatic to serve.

### Got 'em? OKAY, let's do this!

- **Does your DC identify as a specific gender? If so, what gender?**
- **What's the average age of your DC?**
- **Where does your DC live?**
- **Does your DC have a life partner? Children?**
- **Where does your DC shop? Both in person and online?**
- **What types of books, movies, or magazines does your DC consume?**
- **What does your DC do for fun?**
- **What does your DC value more than anything?**
- **What stresses out your DC the most and keeps them up at night?**
- **What does your DC want or crave more than anything?**
- **What are your DC's hopes and dreams? What do they aspire to be?**

Now, this isn't an exhaustive list, but hopefully by answering these questions you're getting a clearer picture of the client you were meant to serve. And ideally, as you do this exercise, you're falling in love with them, at least a little bit.

You see, a lot of people don't take the time to get to know their Dream Client at all. They see them as a paycheck, not a person. I see this tendency more with transactional businesses rather than service businesses, which tend to be more relationship-based.

But our customers are people with hopes and dreams of their own. They also have unique problems that our products and services can solve.

But all too often, they don't know that we have the solution because we're not speaking to them in a way that helps them see it.

This work, getting clear on your Dream Client, is pivotal to a successful business, and it's the primary reason I built my course *The Dream Client Formula*. I saw coaches, consultants, and service-based business owners throwing all kinds of marketing out into the world, but it wasn't connecting. It seemed "salesy" and forced and not at all coming from a place of serving others. In fact, a lot of the marketing I see today seems very self-serving.

But our people are out there and they need us, and *they* are the ones we must step up and serve. If we have a solution to someone else's problem, it is our responsibility to share that solution with them. When we do, they will feel so understood and so "seen" that they will be all too happy to invest in the solution.

If you are looking to attract more Dream Clients (and you should be), I invite you to revisit this chapter once every six months and redo the DC exercise each time. Because here's the thing no one will tell you: **as you grow and evolve, so will your customers**.

When I think back to my first few months of coaching, I was serving women who were making $20,000 or $30,000 per year in their businesses, and some not even that. They experienced Imposter Syndrome and had a lot of issues around being judged. Much of our coaching work was centered around helping them get out of their own way and having the courage to shine!

Now, the women I coach on a one-on-one basis are already making six figures, and most are on their way to seven! They have a strong online presence; many of them are on social media daily. They are comfortable on video because they know it's one of the best ways to connect with their customers (and future customers). They are hosting webinars and launching podcasts . . . they have a wide variety of ways to reach their Dream Client because they know where that Dream Client hangs out online and what they are looking for.

My work is spent helping these women with the big-picture stuff. We look at their overarching annual strategy, leadership skills, and revenue goals (AKA the stuff that moves the needle).

You see, as my own coaching skills have improved over the years, so has the quality of the problem I help solve, and as a result, the caliber of women I serve. The women I coach now are at a different stage in their business. They are focusing on bigger, more complex issues, which I must say, excites me to no end.

You can expect this result too. The person you serve will likely look vastly different in six, twelve, or twenty-four months than they do today. And that's okay. It's a natural part of growth, which is why it's important for you to sit down and do some work on your Dream Client every six months at minimum!

**What about those times you think they're a DC, but they're not?**

Sometimes we want to work with someone so badly that we're blind to certain Red Flags they present with in the initial stages. This situation has sadly happened to the best of us, even me.

One time, in my first few years of coaching, I got an inquiry from a woman I knew and admired. Let's call her "Kylie." She was young, attractive, and had a large social media following. She was an influencer and had a "cool" sense about her. She was also in a very young, hip industry. If I'm being honest, I had a bit of a girl crush on her.

When we first spoke about working together, she rescheduled our call a few times, stating that "life just got busy." No problem, I thought. I'd be happy to connect when it suited her. In our initial conversation, she made it clear that she had certain expectations about working with a coach, and she was looking for someone who fit the bill. We talked about a few ideas and strategies she could try, and she didn't seem too receptive to them. Looking back, I think she expected *me* to do the work for her, which is, for the record, not the job of a coach.

She mentioned a few mutual connections of ours but didn't have anything nice to say about them. In fact, it felt a little like gossip. It made me a bit uncomfortable, but I continued with our conversation because I really wanted a chance to work with her.

Kylie asked what it was like to work with me, and I explained the details of my six-month program. She balked at the price and asked if we could work together for three months instead. I told her that a shortened program was not something I typically did, but I would consider it in this case. She told me she needed to think about it and would get back to me the following week.

*Now, let's play a game called "Spot the Red Flags," shall we?*

To the untrained eye, the above scenario may look like just another sales call, but as someone who now knows better, I can tell you it is a veritable parade of Red Flags.

From the moment we started our conversation, it was obvious she needed to dominate the relationship. She was looking for someone who would do her bidding and with whom she could call all the shots. The very fact that she rescheduled our call multiple times indicated that she didn't respect my time or abilities.

Another Red Flag was that she didn't value my strategic approach, nor did she really seem to understand what I did at all! She wanted someone to do all the work for her while she sat back and collected the profits.

The fact that Kylie was speaking ill of our mutual contacts should have told me all I needed to know about her. I chose to ignore and label it a one-off discretion, but I shouldn't have. I now have a no-gossip policy in my business. End of story.

And the real kicker was asking me to downgrade my services to meet her budget. I have specific reasons why this particular program is six months and not three. She said she wanted to work with me, but she didn't want to do things my way. She tried to haggle with me to get a lower price, which is always a Red Flag in my books.

In the end, I did mistakenly take her on as a six-month client, stating if she was unhappy in any way that we didn't have to continue but that I was sure she'd get more than her money's worth. It should come as no surprise that at the three-month mark she came to me in a huff, stating a whole slew of complaints, none of which were valid.

To make matters worse, I was going through a personal crisis at the time, and all my clients knew about it. My father had been hospitalized quite suddenly, and I was forced to reschedule a few appointments. My family and I were beside ourselves with grief and feared the end was near. Happily and thankfully, he survived, but things had looked very grim.

Every other client of mine completely understood the situation and graciously offered me the time and space I needed to be with my family. Kylie, however, threw my situation back in my face. She said she couldn't tolerate my "lack of attentiveness to her needs," and we parted ways. Ugh. I feel gross just thinking about it.

And the worst part was that I saw it coming. I knew after our very first conversation that she was not a DC and we were not a fit to work together, but I took her on anyway with the hope that I could change her or "make it work." I saw the Red Flags, but I chose to ignore them.

**Trust your gut. It's never wrong.**

If a customer is showing Red Flags, take note of them and do not, under any circumstances, shrug them off. Here are some universal Red Flags to look out for that can show up at any time, in any industry. The earlier you notice these the better, and while they may come up in the initial sales call, we often don't see Red Flags before it's too late.

## Red Flags to Avoid

The potential client . . .

- shows up late to calls and meetings
- sends too many emails/texts at all hours, demanding prompt reply
- has an issue with the price or tries to haggle to get a discount
- asks too many questions, is often confused or overwhelmed
- attempts to negotiate terms of service to suit their whims
- seems to "know it all" and/or speaks down to you
- doesn't see you as the authority
- tells you how to do your job
- is shopping around for the best price
- has demands that don't fit into how you do things
- is rude, abusive, or disrespectful in any way

My friend, you are kind, smart, and amazing at what you do, and you deserve to work with the **very best** clients out there. If someone doesn't fit that description, thank them for their time and wish them well, but they're not for you.

And, to help you even further, I'm including my tried-and-true **Universal Dream Client Checklist**.

## My Dream Client . . .

- behaves in a kind, respectful manner
- asks pertinent questions
- shows up to meetings/calls prepared and on time
- is excited to work with me

- understands and deeply values my services
- understands and respects my terms, policies, and procedures
- pays willingly and on time
- fulfills all duties as a client and holds up their end of the bargain
- is willing to put in the "work" to get results
- is willing and able to refer me to others

The last item is not a must, but again, this is the DREAM we're talking about here. If someone has loved working with you, why wouldn't they send their friends your way?

### Firing a Client

This part is never fun, but it needs to be addressed. Sometimes, clients will choose to leave us. This departure almost always has everything to do with them and nothing to do with you. See it as a learning experience and thank the universe for it, then let them go.

Now sometimes things go awry, and you wish your client would quit, but no matter what, you just can't seem to shake them. I have this amazing friend Maya. She's been in her business a long time and has incredible clients, an award-winning podcast, a growing team, and is seen as an authority in her space. It's safe to say, she's no beginner.

That said, Maya recently came to me and explained that she had to cut a client loose. What started out as a fruitful, mutually beneficial relationship had turned into a needy client who wanted a set of services Maya and her team were no longer suited for. The relationship had ceased to be a win-win, and Maya needed to end things. After many attempts, she finally broke through to this client. They have since parted ways, and Maya is free to focus on her true DCs.

So, if you are ever in the situation where you need to fire a client, don't see it as a failure. See it as an opportunity to move through discomfort toward growth.

If you're not as lucky as Maya, you might be in a situation like our dear Joanne. Remember her from the beginning of this chapter? Perhaps your clients are bullying you or not respecting your boundaries. Perhaps you missed a few Red Flags in the sales phase, and now you're paying for it.

It's okay. Take a deep breath. I've got a four-step framework for you to follow right here.

## "How to Fire a Client" Framework

### Step 1: Address the Issue Openly, In Real Time

Sometimes, a client doesn't realize when they're not holding up their end of the bargain. Other times, they're just crossing their fingers, hoping to get away with it. In any event, schedule a conversation, ideally when you can see their face (so video conference), and let them know what isn't working for you. Speak openly and honestly about your concerns and why you find these acts troubling.

You may wish to make some notes before the call to ensure you don't leave anything out. Delivering negative feedback can be hard, but it's a crucial skill to develop as a business owner.

The real key here is to deliver the feedback "in real time," meaning the moment the issue arises. You're not waiting for some far-off, prescheduled meeting that will take place three weeks from now. You're jumping on a call and getting to the bottom of the issue, pronto.

**Step 2: Correction Period**

If the client is receptive, offer them a "do-over." Suggest a period of time in which you will try to make things work. Let them know the changes you will need to see in order to continue working together, then schedule a meeting to sit down and discuss your progress. The amount of time you give them to course-correct will depend on the nature of what you do, how frequently you have contact, etc., but for most working relationships, two to four weeks should do the trick.

**Note:** If you provide more of a one-off service like a photographer or a makeup artist does, it may not make sense to offer a correction period. Simply finish the work you've been contracted to do and move on.

**Step 3: Firing with Grace**

If you've done Steps 1 and 2 but still don't see a change, it's time to let them go—with love and kindness. Sit down with your client and let them know that you really don't see it working out. In a kind way, explain why this relationship is no longer a fit and that you feel they would be better served by someone else. You can feel free to refer them to another service provider if you wish, but don't feel obligated. After all, if this client is difficult, don't dump them on someone you value and respect or you risk damaging that professional relationship.

Once the conversation is over and arrangements have been made to end your work together, make sure you get all terms in writing.

**Step 4: Cash Out**

In some cases, you may be in a situation where a refund is necessary, in which case it's best to get it over with ASAP. Issue the refund and be sure to send them a statement that captures what has transpired. You will want it for your financial records as well.

**A word of caution:** Please don't make it a habit to issue refunds, and if you must do so, try to keep the amounts as low as possible. It may feel liberating in the moment to throw money at the situation, but if it occurs too often, it can be problematic.

If possible, and only if it makes sense to do so, you can offer a credit to a different offer or service. But if you just want the client gone at all costs, sometimes the only thing to do is to hit them with that refund and be done with them.

And since we're on the topic of moolah, friend, we need to talk. After years of coaching business owners, I can tell you that many of the biggest problems I see stem from our aversion to sales and selling ourselves. But if we don't feel good about generating revenue, it's going to have a negative impact on our business, and it's going to be difficult to experience the joy I know you seek. So even though sales might not be your favorite topic right now, my hope is that we're going to change all that with the next chapter.

# CHAPTER 4

# YOUR JOYFUL SALES

I have a confession to make. The first draft of this book had a glaring, gaping hole in it. I wrote pages and pages on designing a beautiful vision. I went on and on about your Dream Clients. Heck, I even wrote a whole chapter just on "playing," but in its early stages, this book failed to include something super important.

Sales.

At the time of writing this book, I will have spent more than two decades marketing and selling experiences and services. And I would be doing you a disservice if I didn't share some of that wisdom here within these pages.

That said, most women hate the word "sales." I wish that weren't the case, but it has been my experience that the vast majority of female business owners cringe and shudder at the thought of selling. The main reason? We're not good at it. And we're not good at it because we simply haven't practiced enough. That's it!

Think about it. You wouldn't tell your six-year-old that they were bad at riding a bike, would you? Of course not. You'd know that all kids struggle at bike riding to start. You'd explain that riding a bike is something that's hard for everyone, and that it was hard for you when you were a kid. You'd hug them when they fell. You'd kiss their scrapes and help them back onto their bike, reminding them that with time and practice, they'll improve. All they need to do is keep going. Keep applying themselves. Keep showing up.

So why is it we are so kind to our kids (or friends or partners) when they mess up, but we're so hard on ourselves?

If your first sales experience didn't go perfectly, then it stands to reason you might feel a little awkward when it comes to selling. After all, when we sell something, we're asking someone to give us their hard-earned money for something we believe will help them. It's uncomfortable, and there's a whole whack-load of reasons why that is (for more on this topic, see the next chapter).

**Selling is hard. But newsflash: Lots of things are hard at first!**

Convincing someone to trade their dollars for your goods or services may be uncomfortable, but that's no reason to give up hope. In fact, if you're looking for proof that sales is a skill that can be learned, here you go . . .

## My First Sales Job

Remember back in Chapter 2 when I shared a few details about my first sales job? Well, here's the rest of that story. I was twenty-three and finding my way in the world, while figuring out how I fit in at the fancy travel company. But the truth is, I didn't fit in. Not one bit.

For starters, my colleagues were all older and more experienced than I was, and most of them came from wealthy families in posh neighborhoods around Toronto and had attended the finest private schools. It turned out that many of them were family friends of the owner of the company, and the whole environment was quite cliquey.

I, on the other hand, had not gone to private school, nor did I have any powerful family connections. I just sort of fell into the job through a random contact.

Every day I would walk into the glamorous office, feeling like a fish out of water. I would then spend hours on the phone with extremely wealthy and successful people from places like New York and California, attempting to sell them luxury cycling and wine-tasting trips. Needless to say, I had nothing in common with these people. Like ZERO! I had never been on any of the trips I was selling, and I had only been to Europe once—as a *backpacker*!

While I felt totally out of my depth, I had to persevere. I needed this job and the meager salary that came with it.

One day I was having a particularly tough time. Some customers had been snippy with me, and it felt like every sales conversation I had ended in a "no thanks." I was feeling deflated, and I let it affect my work that day. I was moody and grumpy with my customers on the phone.

And my boss noticed.

He called me into his corner office and asked me to close the door behind me. The air inside the room was stale, and his face was somber.

He asked me to sit down. I did so, nervously. I had no idea what was about to come next, but I knew one thing . . . it wasn't good.

He explained that he overheard my last sales call and that he felt I simply wasn't getting the hang of things. He told me that I could stay on in the company in an administrative role, but my days in sales were over.

In a few short, excruciating moments, I was basically fired from my first-ever sales job.

I spent the rest of the day sobbing my heart out, feeling like a total failure, wishing I could go back and just be better at sales. My heart ached with humiliation, knowing that I was *so* bad at my job that someone wasn't even willing to give me a second chance or a helping hand. It was my first real full-time job after graduating, my first big move as a grown adult, and I failed at it. *I just don't have what it takes,* I thought.

Fast-forward to just a few years later, and I had become one of the most successful salespeople on my team at a different and more exciting job. How, you ask? Simple: I learned the tricks of the trade. The very same tricks I am about to teach you in the pages of this chapter.

Here's something that most people don't tell you. We are not born with the ability to sell. Sales is a skill like most things in life, and just like every other skill, sales can be *learned*. If I can learn it, you can too. Keep in mind that I basically flunked out of my first sales role! I was so bad at sales that the company insisted I never speak to another customer again. But if I can go from Sales Flunky to Badass Business Maven in a matter of years, then so can you!

You can be outstanding at sales. But only if you believe that is possible.

And I'll add this point: **being a business owner means being a sales-person**. If you are running a business, dreading the sales part and hoping it will go away, you're not in the right line of work, sadly. Sales and marketing are big parts of running a business, and the sooner you embrace them and find a way to be good at them, the sooner your business will thrive.

## The Difference Between Marketing and Selling

The world of sales and marketing is a big one and can be confusing. I find lots of people are unclear about the difference between sales and marketing. So, I am going to break it down for you here so that it will help you tackle this important area of your business with clarity and ease.

When we have a business, we take our clients on a trip from not knowing us at all, to knowing us a little bit, to liking us, and to eventually trusting us with their business. At least, we should be doing this on the regular. This trip is called the "Customer Journey," and I teach a lot about it in my various programs. I have literally created thousands of hours of content on this subject. But for the purposes of this book, I'll keep it simple.

In order for someone to buy from us, they need to know, like, and trust us. Think about it: **no one buys from someone they don't like or trust**. So, the marketing and sales process is really about taking someone, a stranger at first, on a journey to do exactly that: know, like, and trust us. And if we do things right, this journey ends in a sale! Yay, you!

Let's break it down.

**Marketing** is the process of turning a stranger into a lead. It's how we get someone to notice us and say, *"Hey, I think I might want to do business with her."*

**Sales** is the process of turning that "lead" into a sale or getting someone who is interested in working with us to say, *"Yes, I'm in! How do we get started?"*

In short, we first need to generate enough leads—people who are interested in our stuff—to make enough sales to reach our business goals. When we're not reaching our goals, it can feel super frustrating, especially when we're not sure what the problem is or how to fix it. So, let me help you.

If you are not generating enough leads (i.e., no one seems to know about or care what you do), you have a marketing problem.

If you are generating leads and are connecting with them but no one is buying, you have a sales problem.

Said another way, in order to have a successful business, you must have both strong marketing and strong sales skills. If you are feeling overwhelmed by all this information right now, don't fret. I created a formula to teach people to both attract and convert more of their ideal customers. It's called the Dream Client Formula, and in the next few pages, I'm going to teach it to you.

**Marketing is just speaking directly to your DCs.**

The first step in the Dream Client Formula is your marketing. You need to put out quality content on just a few platforms where your Dream Clients actually hang out. You need to do so regularly and with intention so that your DCs say, "Hey, there's that Lianne girl again. I wonder what she's up to now? She always seems to have something interesting to say."

Here are a few questions to ask yourself as you set out to connect with and attract your DCs:

- **What do I want to be known for?**
- **What makes me different from other people in my space?**
- **What is my DC struggling with?**
- **What do they need to hear from me right now in order to know I can help them?**
- **Where does my DC hang out online?**
- **How often do I need to show up for my DC to get to know me?**

By now you have taken the time to get clear your Dream Client. I'll tell you why I chose these specific points for you to ponder.

- **What do I want to be known for?**

In order for them to buy from you, your DCs must see you as an authority in your space. They must know that you are someone who can get them to where they want to be, so test out different messaging until you find the blend that works for you.

It's simply not enough to say, "I am someone who helps people do XYZ" or "I am an X business owner." The key is to stand out.

You want to be viewed as a leader or expert in your field, someone who not only helps people, but is leading the way in the battle to get from Point A to Point B. I personally want to be known as one of the top female business coaches in the world, and I try to show up that way.

(As an aside, writing this book is one of the ways I have established myself not just as a coach, but as a thought leader. You don't have to write a book, but you do need to know what kind of expert you aim to be and then own that!)

⊚ **What makes me different from other people in my space?**

The whole point of marketing is for you to stand out from the crowd. Make potential clients curious so they stop scrolling long enough to start learning from you. Show them you are the person who can solve their problems, and you'll create a massive connection. Here are a few areas in which you may stand out from the pack:

- Do you have more years of experience in your field (or areas related to your field) than others?
- Do you have any education or credentials in your chosen profession?
- Do you have awards, mentions, or accolades that set you apart?

- Have you appeared in the media for your work?
- Have you established your authority in the form of any publications, books, podcasts, or other forms of credibility?
- Have you worked with any big names in your space, and can you prove that you got them results?
- Can you quantify your results in any way, such as number of clients served, number of dollars raised, number of lives affected by your work? (Tip: Numbers really help build authority.)

⊚ **What is my DC struggling with?** (Note: Revisit your work from Chapter 2)

When you show up in front of your DCs, speak *with* them, not *at* them. Connect with how they are feeling. Deeply understand and speak to where they are struggling and how that feels. You need to help them understand that YOU are the person who can solve their problems, and in order to do that, you gotta speak about their problems.

It may be counterintuitive, but don't be afraid to talk about what's not working in your own journey. People can't connect with those picture-perfect, overly curated personalities we see online that seem to have it all figured out. They want to see our mistakes too. Tell them how you've overcome the situations they are going through and how you help others do the same.

⊚ **What do they need to hear from me right now in order to know I can help them?**

This is quite possibly the most important question when it comes to having a thriving business with happy DCs who feel cared for and served by you. It's not about what *you* want to share, it's about what *they need to feel* that matters most when building a business.

Once you know who your people are and what they are struggling with, it's your duty to ensure they know you are someone who can help them. So how do we do that? We show them that we have been through what they are going through, we understand what it feels like, we know the pain of not being where they want to be, then we show that we know how to get to where they want to be.

A lot of women tell me they struggle with talking about how they can help potential clients because it feels like bragging. I get that feeling, and I have lived that myself. Once I realized that I can't help anyone unless they know I can help them, I realized that by not showing up and sharing my genius, I was keeping myself from living my own mission.

Think about the various ads you are bombarded with on television or online. Do you think, for a second, that those brands feel like they are taking up too much space or "bragging" about their products and services? No way! They show up unapologetically. They shine boldly and share what they have to offer as if it is quite literally God's gift to humanity, and in a way, it is! Their services and products are a gift to someone, not everyone. That someone is their Dream Client.

Speak to your potential client as if you are speaking to your best friend who is going through this problem. Tell them you understand and that you're available for them. Give them encouragement and advice about how they can overcome their problem and then tell them how you can be of service. Do it in your social media posts, your blogs, your videos, and your emails, and I promise you that you'll start attracting those raving fans faster than you can imagine.

For example, the information I share on my podcast and on social media is a blend of inspiration, education, client-success stories, my own successes, my own failures, and my personal life. It's a blend that works well for me, likely because it helps my future customers see me as an authority figure, but also as someone they'd love to shoot the breeze with over a cup of coffee. If you can do both those things, you're nailing social media, in my opinion.

## A note about sharing your personal life online

In this day and age, it seems everyone shows every aspect of their life online. Don't feel like this has to be you. I am very careful about what I choose to share about my personal life, and you should be too.

My general rule is 80/20, meaning that 80 percent of the time I am sharing helpful, business-related stuff, and 20 percent of the time I'm sharing the messy, the personal, the behind-the-scenes stuff. I find that it's this 20 percent that helps me really connect with my audience.

I also have a rule that I won't share anything on social media that might hurt or embarrass anyone, be it a client, my kids, or Yoon. If I think my sharing may make them feel uncomfortable, I do not post it. And I always ask my client's permission before sharing any part of their journey publicly, as that's just the right thing to do.

### ⊚ Where does my DC hang out online?

You don't have to be everywhere, you just have to show up where it actually counts.

Every time I hear someone tell me how they struggle to show up in all the places all the time, and how hard it is to manage so many online platforms, I give them this exact advice:

I recommend having a presence on just two digital platforms, which should be places where your DC spends time. If not, you are wasting your precious marketing energy. For example, if you are all over Pinterest but your target audience is eighteen-year-old frat boys, you're probably missing the mark.

My ideal clients spend time on Instagram and Facebook. They use each platform with slightly different purposes in mind, but they are there, and often for hours a day. I'd be foolish not to share my best content in those two places. On the flipside, I'd be wasting my time sharing that same content on other platforms that cater to a different demographic than mine. This knowledge is a result of many years of social listening, testing, and tweaking.

Don't worry about being everywhere. Pick two platforms and do them really well. If you're new and find digital marketing overwhelming, start with just one platform. I'd much rather see you shine in just one place than be invisible in many.

⊙ **How often do I need to show up for my DC to get to know me?**

This one can be tricky. The last thing I want is for your entire life to be ruled by a grueling social media strategy that takes hours a day to implement. That said, the more you show up online and speak to your DCs and their needs, the faster you will grow.

I resisted showing up for my people for a long time. I insisted that I was doing "enough" and was certain I could build a remarkable brand with just a few minutes on social media per week.

I was wrong.

Ever since I started showing up more online in videos and speaking from the heart, I started seeing my business grow.

At the time of writing this book, I currently release one podcast per week, which gets shared on all my platforms. I try to show up on video at least twice a week. I have two social media accounts (one personal and one for my community) that have multiple image posts per week. Each post is carefully crafted and scheduled in advance to avoid social media burnout, and I spend a few minutes each week engaging with my people in the comments and DMs. We also release a weekly nurture email that goes to our email list. It may sound like a lot but remember that I now have a team of people to help me execute this strategy and I didn't start out here. We built this presence over time.

You need to find the right pattern and cadence that not only attracts the right customers but also fits into your own lifestyle. It's all about finding *your* way, not the way that works for anybody else. Get comfortable with testing stuff out and playing with your marketing until you find the right mix that works for you.

### A note about Imposter Syndrome

Imposter Syndrome is a debilitating condition that stops one from creating the impact they were born to make. It is basically our brain trying to keep us small and safe with thoughts like . . .

*Why would anyone care what I have to say?*
*There's already so many people teaching that.*
*They're so much further along than I am; I'm just starting out.*
*I don't have anything new or important to add to the conversation.*

If you've ever had any thoughts like these, congratulations, you're human! We all have thoughts of Imposter Syndrome that cause us to take pause. But don't let those thoughts stop you from getting your message and your mission out there.

Wherever you are in your business or your given field, just start sharing. You'll find your way eventually. You'll uncover what resonates with your people, but only if you have the courage to get it out there. Don't worry what anyone else is doing, they are not YOU. Your DCs don't care what anyone else has to offer or how they do things. They are *your* Dream Clients, and they care what YOU have to say. So, say it. Help them see you as their "one and only," that you are the person for them, and they will start to come.

## Next Steps: Transformative Experience

Once you are generating attention, the next step in the Dream Client Formula is to take the people you have just attracted through your marketing efforts to the next phase of the journey with you. At this point, you've turned a few strangers into followers, and now we want to turn those followers into genuine interested parties—AKA leads!

The best way I know how to turn potential clients into leads is to invite them to what I call your "Transformative Experience." Now that you have their attention, you want to capitalize on it and turn that attention into interest! In order to do that, you need to **give them a taste of what working with you is like**.

This is precisely how I grew my coaching business in the early days: I drove all over town (and sometimes out of town) to various speaking events. I knew that if I could get business owners in a room with me, I could show them how good I was at helping people grow a business and they'd want to hire me as their coach. Generating leads through public speaking is such a simple concept that it boggles my mind as to why more people aren't doing some version of it.

Your Transformative Experience can be any event that you bring people to that helps them learn from you and solidifies that you are the person they want to help solve their problems. It can be a workshop, a webinar, a signature talk . . . really, anything at all. The two keys are:

1. It's only open to those people who have a specific problem.

2. You address that specific problem in your Transformative Experience.

I call it a "Transformative Experience" because if done correctly, your DC feels like they are *already transforming* just by spending a few minutes with you. They can already feel themselves changing and evolving as a result of the knowledge you share with them in this experience. And if you do your job right, by the end of the experience they should be dying to find out how they can work with you.

Now, I want to make a note here that a Transformative Experience is not a fit for all business types. For example, if you sell a physical product, you may find it more challenging to design an experience that helps people want to take the next step in your journey, but I encourage you to think about how this might apply to your business.

When people feel the results of what your business can do for them, they will naturally want MORE, and that's when you invite them to take the next steps.

## Sales Conversations

If you have done a great job in your Transformative Experience and have really given people that delicious taste of how working with you can change their life, then the rest is easy. We need to invite people to take the next step.

If what you sell is something like a program or course, and if you're very seasoned, you might make an offer right there in the Transformative Experience. After all, if you're a good salesperson, you may have already sold them, and all that's left to do is take their credit card info.

But for most of us, it won't come that easily, and you'll need to invite your prospects to take the next step in the journey. In most cases, the next logical step for them to take is to participate in a Sales Conversation (some people prefer the term "Discovery Call"). If you have them interested at this stage, you need to keep that momentum going and invite them to book in for a Sales Conversation with you ASAP. Let them know that you'd love to learn more about their own personal situation so you can offer a customized solution.

Here are a few questions to ask yourself before a sales call:
- **What do I know about this person and their struggles?**
- **What questions do I need to ask them so they will feel comfortable opening up to me?**
- **How will I make them feel seen, heard, understood, and cared for?**
- **What will I need to show them to see that I am the only solution they need?**

People love to talk about themselves, so getting to spend a few minutes on a video call with you—an expert in your field—should feel like a dream come true, and they should be excited to book a call. If not, take a look at your process and your pitch and see where you can improve.

Incidentally, this is one of the reasons why I love video conversations. You can record them (with the client's permission) and watch them back again and again so you know what to work on for next time.

If the thought of doing a video call is making you cringe, I totally feel you. I recently had an amazing client named Nicole. She is smart, energetic, and very skilled at what she does. But she was bringing in people for Sales Conversations, and they weren't buying. Nicole really wanted to get better at selling. She asked me for advice, and I replied with an ask of my own. In order to provide her with the best possible guidance, I asked her to **record herself on a sales call**, then send it to me for feedback. Nicole really wanted to grow her sales, so even though recording herself felt extremely awkward, she agreed. She recorded her next sales call and sent it to me along with a few thoughts on why she felt she wasn't closing the sale.

Then I asked her this question: "Are these thoughts based on your memory, or have you actually watched the video?" Sure enough, she hadn't sat down to watch it because the thought of doing so made her feel so uncomfortable. But she knew what was on the other side of that discomfort—a successful business! Nicole watched her Sales Conversation and was able to uncover more than a dozen little things she could improve. I added another five to six items to the list that she had missed.

Did Nicole feel like a failure? Far from it! She was now armed with the knowledge she needed to improve her sales and thus grow her revenue, and she is currently doing exactly that in her business.

Remember, if you're not having enough Sales Conversations, it's likely because your marketing or messaging is off or that you're not bringing people into a Transformative Experience so they can get to know, like, and trust you. But if you are generating Sales Conversations and they are simply not converting into paying customers, then it's your sales skills you need to work on. Either way, knowledge is power. If your sales are not where they should be, don't be afraid. Find out why so you can make changes. I promise that you'll be happy you did.

And as my gift to you, I am going to share a few of my tried-and-true questions. Include these in your Sales Conversations and you will start to see massive results.

- **How are things going with [insert area you help people with]?**

This question lays the groundwork for your relationship. In order to know if you can help them, you need to hear their pain points. By asking a nice, broad, open-ended question like this one, they will naturally steer the conversation to what's not working for them. After all, if things were perfect, they wouldn't need you. Don't interrupt. Listen actively. Let them share everything that's in their heart so you can identify what's most important to them, then later reflect that back to them in your offer.

- **If I could wave a magic wand and give you the [insert Desired End Result] of your dreams, what would that look like?**

I call this the "magic wand" question, and the best part about it is that you can apply it to literally anything under the sun you are selling and it works. Whether you are selling a custom-built deck, a piece of software, a high-end coaching program, or a trip to Jamaica, this question works!

Don't assume you know what they want; let them paint the picture for you. After all, a thought is far more effective if someone gets their own versus you planting it in their brain. Encourage them to dream big and really delight in exploring this fantasy. The more vivid their desires, the easier your job of selling to them will be.

- **What do you think you would need to focus on to get to that dream scenario?**

This question illustrates whether they are ready to take any amount of ownership in solving their own problem, and it's particularly insightful for coaches and consultants. Even the best coach on the planet can't help someone if that person isn't committed to helping themselves. It is essential you get them to verbalize their own willingness to do the work. If someone is expecting you to do all the work, thank them for their time, then run for the hills! Don't make the mistake I made with Kylie (Chapter 3). See their reluctance as a Red Flag and move on to someone who is ready to take ownership over this problem.

- **How do you think I might be able to help you achieve those goals?**

This question is not about stroking our own ego, although it might look like that at first glance. It's actually a very strategic way to identify a few key things.

First, it tells you how much they know about you and your business. Their answer will help you understand how much or how little you need to sell yourself, and it also indicates a level of interest in your services.

Next, it shows you if they already view you as the expert. If they say things like "I've heard about you through a few people, have been following you on social media, and recently binged a few of your podcast episodes," you'll know you've established your expertise already. High five, friend!

But if they respond by saying, "I don't know, someone said I should speak to you," and they show little to no enthusiasm for you or your work, it's possible they won't fall into the category of Dream Client, even after your best pitch.

Lastly, this question will help you establish if this person has realistic expectations about their situation and what it will take to overcome it. If the implication is that you will do all the work and can work magic despite any major roadblocks, that's worth knowing at this stage. My hope is that their response to this question is a strong match with how you can see yourself and your team (if you have one) helping them.

⊚ **What are you looking for in a [insert what you do]?**

Again, I ask this question to identify their needs but also to see if it is a match with what I can deliver. It also helps establish expectations for both parties. For example, if I ask someone, "What are you looking for in a business coach?" and they respond with "Someone who I can have daily contact with and 24/7 access to," that's a *hell-to-the-no* for me, and I need to let them know that now. The sooner you establish exactly what you can do for them and how you do that, the better. Set those boundaries early in the journey so you won't end up like sweet Joanne from Chapter 3.

⊚ **What questions do you have for me at this point?**

By this time they should be asking, "How do I work with you?" or some version of that question. If not, you've somehow lost them, and it's your job to figure out how to get them to the point where they cannot wait to hear about your offers!

They may have other questions too, and it's your job to identify if these questions are normal or if they fall into the Red Flag category we talked about in Chapter 3.

Think of it this way: everything they ask or say is giving you a clue into what it would be like to do business with them, so pay close attention.

## Asking for the sale

Once you have someone in a Sales Conversation and it is going well, it's time to ask for the sale. While it may be tempting to play it safe and avoid pitching to this customer, consider all the time and toil that went into attracting this lead, nurturing them with your content, building up that trust and getting them to book this call. It took a lot of energy to get them to this point. Don't waste all that hard work!

If someone likes what you are all about and you think you can help them, you need to tell them so. Make them an offer they can't refuse. Share what product or service you think they'd be a fit for and why. Describe the service, but more importantly, share the results they can expect to achieve if they do invest in you. Don't be shy. You should believe in your offers so strongly that you should be willing to shout them from the rooftop:

"I'M LIANNE, AND I'M AN AWESOME BUSINESS COACH! YOU SHOULD DEFINITELY HIRE ME!"

Okay, I'm exaggerating . . . a little. But you get the picture. When you believe in yourself and the power within you to change lives, then selling is easy. Remember, they came to you because they already think you can help them, so now it's time to affirm those thoughts.

## Don't sell more than one thing

Nothing irks me more than when I want to buy something and the salesperson confuses me by telling me about too many different options. I don't want to know all that! I came to you to tell me what you think will serve my needs. I don't want to choose from a long menu of choices—I want to be told what to buy!

And there's a good chance your customers feel that way too. After a great sales call, don't send them to your website, and don't chicken out and tell them you'll send them a quote. Tell them precisely what you think will serve their needs and then tell them how much it costs.

## Get comfortable talking numbers

The sooner you get comfortable talking about how much your service/product costs, the sooner they will see that confidence in you and be ready to buy. Nothing screams "Don't trust me!" louder than a salesperson who doesn't feel good talking price. After all, if your services work, if they get people results, then it doesn't matter what it costs.

Tell them what the offer is, what it includes, and what it costs. Explain why it will change their life. If you're struggling with your pitch, study it. You can record sales calls using a platform like Zoom or by using the voice memo function on your phone. It will take time and likely several attempts, but trust me, it's worth it. If you do it confidently over a period of weeks, or months, you will improve! Keep recording and reviewing your work until all you hear is 100 percent confidence. That's when you know you've mastered sales!

### Don't backpedal

One of the things that breaks my heart is when a woman is selling me on her services, then shares her price, and before I've had a chance to respond, she starts backpedaling. She starts justifying why she charges what she does, or worse, she offers me a discount before I've even had a chance to respond to the price.

We backpedal out of fear of rejection. We don't want someone to say no to us (and God forbid we make someone feel uncomfortable), so before we can even handle any objections (a vital sales skill), we start discrediting our own worth. We talk ourselves out of the sale. How exactly does one create the impact and earn the income they desire if they continue to play small, shrink their greatness, and discredit their worth every single time they are faced with the possibility of hearing a "no?" They don't. They stay stuck. I want to help you move past that feeling. Nothing sucks worse than staying stuck in the same place year after year, all because you are afraid of pitching yourself and asking for the sale. These are crucial skills that every business owner must learn in order to operate a successful, sustainable business!

Listen, I know talking about offers and money can be incredibly uncomfortable (which is why the entire next chapter in this book deals with money), but don't let this discomfort get in the way of you growing a kick-ass business.

Remember that you are **amazing** at what you do. You help people and people need you, so my hope is that this chapter has inspired you to go out and start reaching and nurturing those people who could really use your help. Don't worry about the ones who don't; they're not your concern.

Just keep your focus on the select few who are worthy of you and value your work. Connect with them and show them why they should choose you. That's all sales really is, and you can do that.

CHAPTER 5

# YOUR JOYFUL MONEY

All right, lay it on me . . . how are you doing so far? I know this book has been a fun ride . . . you're getting clear on who you want to serve and how. If I've done my job right, you're having a grand ol' time dreaming big. Hurrah!

We are now going to shift into an area that a lot of women find challenging to think about, let alone talk about: the dreaded "M word."

That's right, we need to talk about **money**.

I have a lot of experience coaching women through their "money baggage," and to be honest, even after years of doing this work, I'm still not entirely sure why money is such a loaded subject for us, but I'm going to share three of my hypotheses with you here.

### The three reasons women feel uncomfortable with money
**Reason #1: We're not raised to excel at money**
When you were a child, did your parents say to you, "Now, honey, it's important you really learn to understand money and how it works"? My guess is, probably not. In fact, the opposite is likely true.

For most of us, our parents didn't talk about money with us at all. Aside from receiving a modest weekly allowance in exchange for completing household chores, the topic of money rarely came up in conversation in my childhood, and when it did, it was quickly dismissed. My parents never discussed their finances in front of my siblings and me; rather, it was a subject for behind closed doors, as I am sure it is in most homes.

If this is the narrative most children experience when it comes to money, what messages are being received?

- Money is none of my business.
- Money is not something I should think about or ask about.
- Money is something that only adults talk about, and only in secret.
- Money is dark and mysterious.
- Money is not a good thing.

As a result, how are we going to feel about money when that is our experience from a young age?

Another sad fact is that boys seem to have more exposure to money-related concepts like earning money, saving, and investing than girls do. So, when the messaging girls receive is that we shouldn't concern ourselves with money, we have a very strange and foreign relationship with it. We feel **separate** from money, and that separation often leads to confusion and overwhelm when the time comes for us to manage our own.

In fact, it's rare for young adults to have a place where they can learn about money. Wealth building and money management is not taught in our public school system, and it's not something most of our parents teach us either.

What's worse is that we take on endless student loans to obtain an education, yet nobody educates us about money management! Does anyone else see the irony here?

If no one is teaching us how to create financial freedom, where are we supposed to learn it?

We are forced to fend for ourselves when it comes to our financial education, and therefore, we feel lost in a big, complex world we know nothing about. As a result, many women opt out, often leading to tragic situations such as facing mountains of debt, having bad credit and thus unable to get a loan or a mortgage, and living paycheck to paycheck. Something has to change.

**Reason #2: We hand our money power over to men**
Because we come from a background where most women are not taught the value of money and how to earn more of it and build it, we then grow up to find life partners who seem to know more about it than we do.

Let me stress that this is not always the case. But in most intimate relationships, one partner tends to embody more feminine energy (usually the homemaker/caregiver) and the other more masculine energy (the breadwinner).

Despite the fact that most women now work and generate an income, those societal norms have not changed much over millennia.

Plain and simple, when we partner up, many of us turn our "money power" over to our masculine counterparts, who then manage the household finances.

Again, this is not the case in all partnerships. But in my coaching work, I have seen this scenario more often than not. Money is something stressful, confusing, and best handled by someone other than ourselves, so we hand over the responsibility to the partner who seems more adept at it.

**Fun Fact:** My own parents started out this way. My dad handled the money stuff for many years until my mom finally stated that she felt she could do a better job managing the family finances. So, she took it on and has held that position ever since.

I'm not saying she is better at it, because I honestly don't have that intel, but I will say that in all these years, I have never seen them fight about money. Not once. They have both been happily retired for the last twenty years, surviving multiple economic crises while still enjoying all the things they love. My guess is that whatever their system is, it's working!

In my household my husband manages the investing, but I manage my business finances (naturally) and track our dollars in and out every month. It's a team effort in this house.

I feel every household must make these decisions for themselves. But what I'd like to see is more women stepping into their power and taking on more financial responsibility. Rather than blindly handing over financial control to our partners, I want us to take responsibility to educate ourselves about money, how it works, and especially, how it can grow by making smart choices.

**Reason # 3: Money (and math) seem hard**

I've touched on this reason in the previous paragraphs, but for many of us, somewhere along the lines, we decide that money seems hard and therefore, we simply wash our hands of it. We check out. I saw this happening with many of my female friends at an early age. Again, they weren't taught simple investing strategies from parents, teachers, or mentors, so they assumed money was an area they're "just not good at" and decided not to invest their own time and energy into *becoming* good at it.

When something feels hard to do, how excited are we to take a stab at it? Not very!

Money is closely linked with mathematics, a school subject that many girls receive little encouragement in. Want proof? How many female engineers or math professors do you know?

As a young girl, I recall some of my relatives saying things like "the women in this family just aren't good at math." What do you think was the result of that narrative? I, of course, started to adopt the same belief, probably because a) it seemed true, and b) I likely craved a sense of belonging, as we all do.

In elementary school I was strong in subjects like language, art, and music, but math and science were subjects I struggled with continuously. As time went on, I naturally leaned into the areas I felt more confident in, and as a consequence, I paid less attention to anything to do with numbers. **Math made me feel stupid, so I avoided it**.

While I did struggle in math class throughout all elementary school, the good news is that when high school came, I decided to turn things around. I got extra help from my teachers and worked with a tutor so that I could graduate with a decent grade.

And here's the best part! Once I started making and saving my own money, math actually started to make sense!

I worked on my personal finances in my twenties when I was just starting to earn my first grown-up salary. This work allowed me to purchase my first home by the age of thirty-two on my own, without the help of a spouse. I'm not suggesting home ownership should be the goal, but financial empowerment should be.

**IMPORTANT:** If you have experienced any ill feelings toward money, be it earning it, saving it, or spending it, please keep paying special attention to this chapter!

So, what if money didn't have to be hard? What if we could feel amazing about our money? Well, I believe that is possible, and it starts with examining the Three Pillars of Financial Freedom I discuss in this chapter.

While I'll be discussing business finances primarily, I want you to know that even if you don't have a business yet, these are sound strategies that apply to personal finance as well. There's a lot more to financial fitness than I have space for in this book, but the truth is that most of us aren't even doing the basics! Master these fundamentals first and then you can move on to more complex concepts.

## Financial Freedom Pillar #1: Know what you have

One of the toughest moments for me working with a client is when I ask what is seemingly a very simple question, and I get a very troubling answer.

The question: *How much are you currently earning in your business?*

The answer (often coming after a few moments of stalling, apologizing, justifying, and self-flagellation): *I don't really know.*

How is it that these remarkable, badass women are starting and growing world-changing businesses, generating thousands (sometimes even millions) in revenue, reaching and serving massive audiences, writing books, launching movements, and essentially changing the friggin' world, how is it these same women can have no clue what's in their bank account?

Here's my take. Many women start a business with the aim of changing lives. They start a venture that they are passionate about, that uses an immense amount of their creative genius, and they put the emphasis on "helping others." I get it! We all want to make the world a better place. I'm right there with you!

But sadly, they are not paying themselves in a systematic way. They are skimming a little here, a little there. They often don't separate out their business earnings from their personal finances, which creates a dangerous gray area. They don't know where the business revenue ends and their own money begins. They know they should do something about it, but they continue to tell themselves, *"Money is hard."*

The cycle continues as they grow and scale.

The strongest, most solid businesses last beyond the first year or two (yay!), and they continue to thrive. They have a sound business model, and their clientele are happy and thus, sending more referrals. They gain traction. The business grows, and they may need to bring on staff to help them continue on this trajectory. They want to maintain this growth pattern, so they continue to spend money on the things that will help them grow (often advertising, systems, staff), so their expenses increase. But they still have no clue about a few basic factors, notably what's coming in, what's going out, and what's left over at the end of the day.

By now they might be earning multiple six figures. They may have outsourced the "money stuff" to an accountant or a bookkeeper (or both) so they can focus on the tasks they enjoy more. (Outsourcing, in theory, is not a bad thing; however, outsourcing any area of our business without first understanding it can have disastrous effects on our business and bottom line.)

By this point, they feel at ease because at least the money stuff is getting done by *someone*. But they've extracted themselves from the process. They approach money with a "not my problem" attitude. Managing the money is the job of someone who is not actually running the business at all, but by some stranger who gets paid by the hour.

It's not unusual for women to be several years into their venture only to find they are not paying themselves (or at least not well). They are unclear how much they are earning, and what they're earning is simply not enough to live the life they want.

**It's time we stop this madness and start getting a handle on the money side of our businesses!**

It's time we take the financial health of our business into our own hands and get a clear picture of what's *really* going on so we can make informed decisions that increase our profits and peace of mind.

If you haven't done this work (or haven't done it for a while), it can feel super daunting. But fear not. I've coached hundreds of women on the financial aspects of their business, and I can safely say that it's not rocket science. Many of us make it out to be harder than it actually is.

That's why step one to gaining financial clarity—and frankly financial happiness—is to understand what is happening right now in your business. One of the easiest ways to find out is to start by looking at where you track dollars that come into the business and dollars that go out of the business. This might be:

- your annual tax statement
- your accounting/invoicing software
- your PayPal or Stripe account
- your e-commerce platform

If you have multiple ways of accepting payment, you may need to look in all those places. For example, in my company we currently accept payment in two ways: 1) clients pay their invoices through Quickbooks, and 2) clients purchase our digital offers through our e-commerce site. So, at the end of the month, those are the only two places money is entering the business.

If you don't know where money is entering your business, we have a bigger problem. But I am assuming if you have a legitimate business whereby people are purchasing products and services and paying you with money for those items, you know how they are paying you.

When was the last time you looked at the gross revenue earned in your business (that is every penny that comes into the business excluding any sales tax)?

One month ago? Six months ago? Over a year? If it has been a while, it stands to reason you may feel *very* disconnected from your money. But that's okay. It's better to know what we're dealing with now, so we can make the necessary changes.

Go ahead and take a few moments to open your bank accounts or accounting platforms and do a quick search of how much was sold in the last twelve months.

Don't worry, I'll wait.

Once you know your gross revenue, here comes the hard part. You might like what you see (I sure hope that's the case), but you might not. I want you to know that whether you look at that number and feel a sense of pride or a sense of something more like humiliation, there's always hope.

Don't like what you see in the bank account? Great news! You can change it! But it starts with knowing and understanding what is really going on.

If you've ever been on any sort of weight-loss program, this analogy might help. What's the first thing you do when you start a weight-loss journey? You get clear on your current status. You step on that scale, look at the number, and accept it. You don't have to like it, but you do have to accept it.

After that is done, we can start to think about goals. These programs typically help you decide upon your "goal weight." For any transformation to take place—physical, financial, or otherwise—we need to know two important details:
Point A: Where we are right now.
Point B: Where we want to be.

The journey, the transformation, happens as you move between Point A and Point B, and the joy comes as you see yourself making progress toward your desired destination.

This progress is important because it's what keeps us motivated to continue on this path to change. To gain more financial clarity, to have more money, and to enjoy that money more, we must first understand where we are at.

While I think bookkeepers and accountants are helpful, they are not our CFO, and they are not committed to helping us achieve financial success (at least most of them are not). Financial professionals are tools that can help us gain clarity in the financial health of our business, so use them, but with caution. Make sure you know exactly what you want an accounting professional to help with in your business. Tell them where you're struggling to gain more clarity and ask them for the specific help you need to fix this problem.

I had been using a bookkeeper who provided me with a simple Profit and Loss (P&L) statement by the fifteenth of each month for the month prior (if you are using a bookkeeper, I recommend they provide you with your reports on a monthly basis, and with a quick turnaround).

I was gaining clarity on my earnings, my expenses, and my profit on a monthly basis, but over time, more clarity was needed. I now request this report monthly, plus two others: P&L year-to-date and P&L for the last twelve months consecutively. That way, every thirty days I get the most accurate picture of the financial health of my business.

If I don't like what I see, the power is in my hands to change it, and that's where we are going to go next.

### Financial Freedom Pillar #2: Be intentional about earning

Remember when I shared with you how my Strategy Jams work—that women join me for a day of dreaming and planning? This is often the hardest question for them to answer:
*How much do you want to be paying yourself?*

I frequently hear answers like . . .
*"I don't know, a lot?"*
*"What's a reasonable salary?"*
*"How do other people answer this question?"*
*"I want to make what I made in my old day job; is that good?"*

What do you notice about each of these replies? I'll give you a hint: they all end in a question mark.

It is extremely rare for a client of mine to reply to this question with a clear and definitive number that they have given thought to and feel amazing about. It has happened a handful of times in my coaching career, at most. The agonizing reality is, just as we shy away from dreaming big when defining our big vision, we do the same thing when it comes to our money.

Part of our inability to dream big about money is due to what we talked about earlier: that women are not taught to manage it. And the other part of the problem is that we have no frame of reference. We don't know what is possible, and therefore, how can we decide what's possible for us?

What if I told you that anything is possible? That any amount of money you want to earn in your business—the sky's the limit!—is absolutely possible?

I firmly believe that we can achieve any amount of revenue we want, but it won't matter one bit until we get clear on *why* that is important to us!

Want to make a million dollars? Fabulous! Now tell me why that matters. How will earning a million dollars change your life? How will it allow you to feel more joy? If you can't answer those questions, a million dollars is likely not the right number.

Knowing your "why" is exactly the reason I often start with defining our own personal salary. After all, a business can generate $1,000,000, but if $999,999 of it goes toward expenses, and you keep none of it, then what the hell is the point?

Money is only meaningful when we make it meaningful, which is why I think most women relate their dream salary to something they are already familiar with—for example, what they earned in their old job.

I did the same thing. When I left the corporate world, I was making about $80,000 a year. Incidentally, this was the most money I had ever made in a one-year span in my entire life. My average annual salary up until that point was closer to $45K/year, so needless to say, earning "good money" was a very new feeling for me.

But here's what I knew: I wasn't quitting my job so I could make *less* money than what I was making there. Quite the opposite. I was leaving my job so that I could *increase* my earning potential!

During this time of transition, Yoon and I had many difficult discussions about this topic. I found it challenging because the truth was, I had no actual proof that my business would work. I longed for financial success and was working toward it, but most of my plans were based on pure faith.

I asked Yoon to have that same faith in me.

I asked him for his full, unconditional support, and in return, I would do my best to build a successful business and meet or exceed my old salary within two years. And then I added that if I couldn't make it work within two years, I would go out and get a sales job.

It was a promise I made to him, mostly to hold myself accountable to my own financial goals. The last thing I wanted to do at that time was to go back to working for someone else. Suffice it to say, that was all the motivation I needed.

So, my "why" became very clear. I was focused on making $80,000, and yet at the same time, I started to realize that the real goal, the *why* behind $80,000, was so my family wouldn't feel any pain as a result of my decision to quit my stable job—we would still have all the same things, enjoy all the same experiences, go on all the same trips, and enjoy all the same programming. In my mind, my *why* was so that I could still support my family without our finances taking a hit due to my choice to have more professional freedom.

I started earning $3K per month, then $5K, then $7K. Pretty soon, I was well on track to hit my $80K-per-year goal.

And then something major happened.

I was coaching a client of mine named Lois who is a talented interior designer and also notably shy and introverted. She was newer to running her business full time and was struggling with confidence and owning her worth, as many of us do in the early days. She was pretty green when it came to setting clear financial targets. But one day, in a moment of extreme clarity in the middle of a coaching session, she sat up straight and declared, "I want to make six figures this year. I'm going to do it!"

I was completely blown away by her commitment, but at the same time felt a sense of lack in my own convictions. If this woman, a woman *I* was coaching and who certainly was not as strong in sales or marketing as I was, could effortlessly declare her plan to earn $100,000 that year, why couldn't I?

When she left the session, I pulled out my financial targets I had set for the year and proceeded to increase them. I, too, would make $100,000 in my business that year, my first year as a self-employed individual.

How would I do it? I wasn't sure, but I knew that the first step was **believing it was possible**. After all, what did I have to lose?

As it turns out, Lois did hit six figures that year, and so did I. In fact, I did it in the first nine months. And once I reached that milestone, I had a massive aha moment. I had been holding myself back from achieving my full financial potential. I had been playing small, setting safe, attainable goals so I could feel accomplished, but at the same time was capable of much, MUCH more. Once I hit six figures in nine months, I knew anything was possible if I got intentional about it.

So, my friend, have you been **intentional** with your business earnings? If so, congrats! You're in the minority, though.

If not, why not? Does earning "good money" feel impossible? Does it feel selfish? Does it feel too complicated? Does it feel meaningless or shallow?

If it feels like any of these things, you're not alone. Most women who struggle to set clear and compelling financial goals do so not because of a lack of smarts or resources. They struggle because of the voices in their own head—their inner "mean girl."

Here's a list of things I have heard women say when they speak about money:

*"But if I want that, isn't that greedy?"*

*"It's in my DNA. My parents weren't wealthy, and I won't be either."*

*"I really don't need to make that much. I'm happy just getting by."*

*"I don't want to be superficial. To me, the money isn't as important as making a difference."*

*"I am in a helping profession. The goal shouldn't be to make a lot of money, it should be to help people."*

*"I've never been good with money."*

If your heart sank a little while reading those statements, now you know how I feel on a regular basis when my women open up to me about their thoughts and feelings toward earning abundantly. But it doesn't have to be that way. I'm going to ask you a few questions right now that I want you to ponder and have the courage to answer honestly.

- **If anything were possible, how much money would you make?**
- **If you didn't have to worry about what others thought, what would you like to earn?**
- **What salary would make you feel so freakin' amazing?!**
- **If you could do amazing work, helping others *and* being well paid, what would you earn?**

⊙ **What amount of money would indicate to you that you were making the impact you were born to make?**

⊙ **If you gave yourself permission to earn what you are really worth, what number is that?**

At the end of the day, money, your salary, is just that: a number. Stop creating so many stories about it and start getting intentional.

How much do you want to earn in the next twelve months? Look at your answers to the previous questions as a starting point.

Next, how many customers would you need to serve to earn that amount, and in what ways? What needs to change for you to earn that amount? Do you need to raise your rates? Do you need to serve more people? Do you need to create new offers or adjust your current ones?

Want to know a secret? When it comes to generating revenue, there are only so many ways to get the job done. You can:

1. Get more customers
2. Get those customers to buy more often
3. Create more things to sell
4. Increase your prices

Ta-da! If you want to earn more in your business, it's not all that complicated, but you will need to put some thought and likely planning into how it will happen.

Stop waiting to be worthy and wishing things were different. Start claiming your power and owning your worth. Stand strong in your gifts.

Want to earn more? Intend it, damn it. Demand it. Declare it like my sweet client Lois did, and it will start to happen for you. But it won't happen by accident or luck. It will happen because you've made the empowering decision to create a salary that allows you to live the life that you want.

### Financial Freedom Pillar #3: Be mindful with spending

*How much should I be spending in my business?*

If I had a nickel for every time someone asked me that question! I wish I could say there was just one clear answer. The truth is, it depends on a lot of factors like whether you are a product-based business, if you own or rent a physical space, your staffing needs, and if you're currently in growth-mode.

Essentially, there is no set prescription on how much any one business owner should be spending in their business to achieve the goals they want to achieve. But what I can say is, it is less than 100 percent of what you bring in. Much less.

The issue isn't that women are overspending or underspending or even spending on the "right" or "wrong" things. The main issue is they have *no clue* how much they are spending. They're simply not tracking these key metrics I've been talking about: 1) What's coming in? 2) What's going out? 3) What's left over at the end of the day?

To use another weight-loss analogy, what's one of the most effective methods for someone to lose weight? It's to track how much they are consuming on any given day (calories in) and how much energy they expend in that same day (calories out). If you want to lose weight, you start paying attention to what you can eat and how much you move. And countless systems, programs, and apps exist to help the hordes of weight-loss seekers with this monitoring every single year, which is one of the reasons that weight loss is a trillion-dollar industry.

**The reality:** We know what to do, we just aren't doing it.

Incidentally, one of my biggest pet peeves is when people claim the reason why they're not further ahead with any given goal is that they don't have the right plan, system, or app to implement the changes they want to make. They are looking for someone to hand them the magic formula or secret tool that will help them crack that code.

I'll let you in on a little secret. I was not happy with my weight for many years. I gave myself all kinds of reasons why I wasn't the weight and shape I wanted to be. They looked like this:

*"I've had two kids; of course I am not going to look like I did in my twenties."*

*"I'm middle-aged; I look better than most of the moms out there my age."*

*"Most people naturally gain weight over time; it's just a fact."*

*"I like food, and I don't want to deprive myself of eating what I love."*

But the cold hard truth of why I wasn't losing weight was that I wasn't actually *trying*. I'd work out hard for a few weeks and then cave when I hit a roadblock. I'd eat healthy for one whole week and then sabotage my efforts come Saturday night in the name of "giving myself a treat."

The real problem was twofold:

1.  I wasn't being mindful about what I was putting in my body. I was consuming too many calories for my frame, often mindlessly eating because my kids were or my husband was, and I was consuming a lot of foods that I know to be harmful to my personal physique (namely wheat, dairy, and processed foods).

2.  I became complacent with my exercise. I was mindful enough to move my body every day, but I wasn't breaking out into a good sweat often enough. In fact, I started making excuses as to why I wasn't challenging myself as much as I once had. On my daily runs, I was moving at a pace one could barely call a jog. Actually, a "wog" would be a more accurate word because while technically I was jogging, my pace was more like a walk.

So, I fell into the classic trap, and I spent countless attempts seeking out this system or that food or this fitness routine that would be that magic bullet for me. *If I only had "X," I would be the shape that I wanted.*

I'll fast-forward to the end of this story because frankly, this is not a weight-loss book and you don't need to hear about my health woes. I recently lost ten pounds at the time of writing this chapter. How'd I do it?

Simple. I started tracking my calorie intake for a period of two weeks. I entered everything I ate into an app that calculated the total number of calories I consumed each day, and in order to hit my goals, I had a range in mind that I aimed for each day that was significantly less than what I had been consuming beforehand.

Next, I started challenging myself from a fitness perspective. I focused on two goals: 1) hitting eleven thousand steps each day, and 2) running for thirty minutes and increasing the intensity with each workout.

So, in essence, I decreased input and increased output. I tracked it, and I measured my results, which was the real key. I created a simple grid in a Word document on my computer that contained 7 x 26 boxes, one box for every remaining day of the year at that time and printed it off. I decided that my goal was to simply fill in the box with my weight each morning.

It was important not to stress about it or judge myself for the results. In fact, with any sort of habit change, it's best when we take the emotion right out of the equation. My objective was to stay on track with my eating and fitness goals and simply write down what I saw on the scale each morning into a tiny box on a paper on my office bulletin board.

The results: The numbers kept getting smaller and smaller until I hit my goal weight and have since then leveled off. Not only was this tool effective for helping me lose those pesky ten pounds that I had been carrying around for, get this . . . *eight years*, it also helped me keep them off and stay within my goal range.

The moral of the story: **Set intentions and measure your success in any area where you want to see change.** Bonus points if you can do so without blaming or shaming yourself but rather celebrating yourself for any (and I mean ANY) progress you make.

Is there one magic way to track your finances? A magical tool that will unlock financial success for you? No, there is not. There are a million ways to do it, so I encourage you to find a way that works for you and commit to sticking with it for a specific timeline. How will you pay yourself what you deserve?

**Step 1: Decide upon the salary that you want to pay yourself.**
**Step 2: Track your income and ensure you're earning enough to pay yourself.**
**Step 3: Track your expenses and ensure you're keeping enough to pay yourself.**
**Step 4: Pay yourself.**

Yes, it's that simple. Does it get more complex as you grow? You bet your ass it does, but for many beginner business owners, these steps are a perfect place to start.

Not sure what system to use or can't find one that works for you? MAKE one! Sometimes the best tracking systems are the ones that come from within because we know how our brain thinks and what it needs to see.

Over the years in business, I've had countless recommendations from mentors and peers about this system or that method or this tool, and when I investigated it, it just didn't work for me. Why? Because I am a special snowflake, and my mind thinks in a unique way. I'm highly creative and visual and therefore, the systems I use really need to be laid out in the way my brain works.

For example, when you think of visualizing your "year," what do you visualize? I visualize a circle where January is at the bottom and July is at the top. And I'm not alone. I've encountered many others who also envision their year as a similar circular image.

How do you visualize your "week?" I envision a series of vertical columns, side by side, where Monday is at the left and Sunday is on the right. It's no surprise, therefore, that my favorite planner is laid out this way.

**My point:** Find what works for you and the way you think. Get clear on the financial metrics YOU need to track for your own clarity and start tracking them. If you can't find a system to track that you like, make your own. And for God's sake, stop stalling and start tracking!

By now you have a sense of how passionate I am about taking control of our business finances. There is absolutely no reason why you should not have clarity over what your business is generating, what you're spending, and how much you are personally keeping. If you ONLY track these three metrics, you are better off than 90 percent of small business owners out there. But as you grow, you'll likely want and need to have a more detailed clarity on your numbers.

After working with countless female entrepreneurs on the money side of their businesses—money mindset and tangible numbers and metrics—I can tell you that there is a direct correlation between how much clarity you have about your finances and how much joy you experience. After all, no one can feel happy when they are living in the dark, scared of their bank statement, drowning in debt, and paying themselves only pennies every month. Nope, that's certainly not my definition of joy.

In fact, when it comes to finances, I believe there are just four factors that are the top indicators for happiness.

### Factor 1: Clarity

When this factor is in check, we feel like we know how much money we have, where it's coming from, where it's going to, and where it currently resides. We have a strong sense of our money and how it works inside our business. Yay!

### Factor 2: Current Earnings

When we have this factor down, we feel we're currently paying ourselves well while doing meaningful work. We feel that sense of pride and accomplishment for our ability to make a good living doing what we love.

### Factor 3: Potential for Growth

With this factor we recognize that while we are comfortable now, there is room for more. We see new opportunities to increase revenue and profits all the time, and we are constantly exploring those opportunities. We don't shy away from new offers or collaborations that might be fruitful for fear of failure. We anticipate the numbers on our P&L will grow over time. In short, we are expecting and planning for growth.

### Factor 4: Return on Investment (ROI)

At this juncture, we're spending on our business, but the spending is in check and feels vital to our continued growth. We're not simply flushing our money down the toilet. Every expense is an investment in our potential growth, and we are tracking our return on investment. If we see an investment is not generating a return, we have options: stop investing in that area, redirect funds to another area, or keep investing in that area but change strategy.

When you build a joyful business, you experience more:
- wealth
- abundance
- clarity
- potential
- prosperity
- success
- gratitude
- generosity

And less:
- scarcity
- confusion
- overwhelm
- guilt/shame
- failure
- fear
- doubt

So, I'll ask you now, do you feel more aligned with the words on the first list or the second? If you answered the first, congrats! You are in a positive place when it comes to money, and while you may need to make a few tweaks to optimize systems, you're living that joyful business we all want.

If you're more in the second-list camp, fear not, my friend! Reading this chapter is a beautiful first step toward financial abundance. Do you know how many problems or challenges I have faced that I *knew* I needed to change but failed to take any action on? Too many to count! The first step to solving any problem is realizing you have one. From there you can make a plan to tackle it. Let this book be your first step. Let me ask you this question:

Which factor do you need to improve?
**Factor 1: Clarity**
**Factor 2: Current earnings**
**Factor 3: Potential for growth**
**Factor 4: ROI**

Or is it a combination of these factors? Whatever your answer, again, knowing is half the battle.

Promise me something, friend. You're not going to beat yourself up because your current finances are not where you want them to be. No, you are far too smart and strategic for that.

Use this book as a guide and decide where you need to take action. For example, if it's Factor #1 you're struggling with, it might be time to hire an accountant or bookkeeper and start reviewing your P&L monthly. Factor #2 not in check? Maybe you need a plan to start paying yourself more (this plan typically requires you to earn more, spend less, or both!). You get the picture.

My friend Lea has an expression: Puzzles, Not Problems. I used to hate problems in my business. I used to feel drained when I thought about the challenges I was experiencing and saw them as frustrating obstacles standing in the way of the growth I desperately craved.

But Lea explained that problems are just puzzles for us to solve and doing so is the work of an entrepreneur. We are supposed to encounter things that require figuring out. After all, if you wanted a manual of how to do your job, it's called the *Employee Handbook*. **But you're not an employee, you're the C-E-friggin'-O!**

You're doing something brave and different, that not many people do, so you will face stuff that most people don't face! And if you're looking for the step-by-step roadmap to success, good luck. You'll probably be looking for a long time. So, take charge of your life, your business, and your finances. Put on your CEO hat, and by all means, ask for the help you need, get resourceful, and figure out how to solve those puzzles with grace, patience, and a little laughter.

**P.S.** If you're looking for a guide to help you create the life and business of your dreams, keep reading. In the next chapter we explore how to create your Dream Schedule.

CHAPTER 6

# YOUR JOYFUL SCHEDULE

I love what I do. Truly. I'm not just saying that. I don't just "like" it. I am all-out, no-holds-barred, head-over-heels in love with my job. But there was a time when that wasn't the case—my first year in business.

To be clear, I loved most things about that first year. I was excited to finally be doing work I found meaningful, I loved making new connections and learning new things, and nothing, I mean *nothing*, beats the thrill of a sale when you're new.

But within six months of this new entrepreneurial life, I hit a wall. I was running out of hours in the day, which hardly felt possible because I was so good at time management! After all, I've been scheduling my life since I was fourteen! I teach this stuff! How could I be failing at time management?!

The embarrassing truth was that I wasn't practicing what I preach.

I had let those dreaded OPAs (remember those from earlier?) start dominating my calendar. I had taken on some safe and predictable contract work, but it was eating up two of my five working days each week (and let's just say, I didn't exactly find this contract work "blissful").

I was seeing my coaching clients three days a week (Mondays, Wednesdays, and Fridays), and I had no booking system, which meant I was manually scheduling every coaching call and entering it into my calendar. If clients needed to cancel or reschedule, they emailed me. I would then send them a list of alternate times to choose from, often resulting in a lengthy game of "email tag." I let this nonsense go on for a year! Frankly, even as I write this, I'm embarrassed it went on for as long as it did.

Another bad habit I'd picked up was switching from task to task with very little rhyme or reason. If something showed up as a to-do, I simply stopped whatever I was doing and started tackling that new task. If I got an email, for example, I'd immediately respond to it.

Each day I would go from managing my inbox, to sending out an invoice, to scheduling a call, to jumping on social media, to coaching a client . . . and that was just in the *first hour*!

I was living in a constant state of panic, like if I didn't take care of a specific task right away, I would forget about it and it wouldn't get done. The fallout was not good. I was on edge. I felt like I was constantly starting and stopping important projects in favor of more trivial yet seemingly essential tasks.

In hindsight, I was just so damn excited to finally be building my own dreams that I was firing on all cylinders—all hustle, no intention. I was constantly bursting at the seams with new ideas, but I had no time to fully implement them. My schedule was a disaster, and that's putting it kindly. THERE WAS NO SCHEDULE! Each day was a flurry of unrelated tasks, each one more scattered and disconnected than the last. I was in constant motion, which made it feel like I was getting shit done, but in reality, I was just running in circles.

And then, I hit burnout.

In the summer of my first year, I became extremely exhausted and caught a bug of some sort. I was experiencing aches and chills and couldn't get out of bed. I took several days off so I could rest. I stopped communicating with my family because my brain was fried. I spent days locked in my room alone. Worst of all, I had no one I could talk to about it because I didn't have a support network that understood what I was going through. I had gone from crushing it in my first six months in business to overwhelmed and bedridden. I was ashamed of burning out so quickly. I knew something had to change.

Turns out, lots of things had to change.

In this chapter I share with you my Seven Pillars for mastering your schedule so that you can get your most important tasks done effectively and efficiently and still have time for the things you love outside of business.

### Pillar #1: Have a Clear Vision

The first step to getting more done is to know *what* you want to get done. It may seem obvious, but it's actually quite critical.

When I coach my women, I learn that they are getting lots of things done, just not the right things. They are extremely busy; in fact, many don't stop moving all day long. They're always *doing*, but they're not feeling fulfilled because the things they are accomplishing have no significance.

The good news for you, my friend, is that you already did this work back in Chapter 1 when I asked you to create your compelling Five-Year Vision. Right on!

So long as you completed those exercises, you already have a strong sense of where you want to be in five years' time, and that vision now becomes an anchor that grounds you, especially when things get challenging, which they will. Once we are clear on our 5YV, we can break it down into more short-term, concrete goals.

### Pillar #2: Know What You Want to Get Done

When you look at your 5YV, it may seem scary as hell, and you may be having thoughts of *Oh dear God, how am I going to get there?* If you haven't had those kinds of thoughts, you're either not thinking big enough or you are a robot. In any case, check yourself and your vision before proceeding.

You don't have to know all the steps right now. I am going to ask you to think of just three tasks—three things that if completed in the next ninety days would bring you infinitely closer to achieving your Five-Year Vision. These are your three **Desired End Results** (or DERs, as I like to call them).

Here are a few examples of what I'm talking about:

If your 5YV is to become a well-known author in the personal-development space (move over Rachel Hollis!), your DER might be to write a first draft of your first book by a certain date.

If your 5YV is to have a $1M online-learning business, perhaps your DER is to launch your first course.

If your 5YV is to be a thought leader in the wellness space, perhaps your DER is to host your first workshop.

Your DER doesn't have to be an earth-shattering one, but it should be something that:

- lights you up
- is in line with your 5YV
- can be completed in ninety days
- is big enough that it will require a significant amount of focus
- will make an impact in your business

If your DER is not meeting those requirements, it's likely not the right DER, and you need to dig a little deeper.

Incidentally, when I do this work inside A-Players, my ninety-day group-coaching program, a lot of the women struggle with finding the "right" goal, so I work with them to fine tune their vision and help them select the DER that's meaningful to them and in line with their mission.

So, if you're struggling to land on the right DER, you're in good company. Trust you will figure it out!

I use the term "Desired End Result" because the word "goal" is grossly overused and often misused. Plus, it seems everyone in the personal-development space talks about "goal setting," but very few of them talk about "goal getting." We're great at setting goals but seem far less concerned with actually achieving them.

That's why I like the term "Desired End Result." It forces one to think about the specific end result they want to achieve versus some general area of focus.

Therefore, when you are in your next ninety days, what are some of your DERs? If you were to set some intentions—results you plan to achieve in three months—what would they be?

**DER #1: What is the number one thing you want to accomplish in the next ninety days?**

**DER #2: If you were to complete your first DER, what would be the next thing you'd like to achieve?**

**DER #3: In a perfect world, if you could accomplish three outstanding results in the next ninety days, what would be the third?**

You'll notice that I didn't put the same weight on these three DERs, and that's because not all goals are created equal. In my coaching programs, I always ask women to select their primary DER, the one thing they will accomplish above all else. This request forces them to prioritize based on what matters most to them.

The mistake I see often is that people place equal weight on all goals and then put themselves in a state of stress chasing many of them at once. When you prioritize your goals, you work toward your primary goal first and foremost. Once that goal is checked off the list, only then do you move on to the next, and so on.

Sometimes, your DERs seem to prioritize themselves based on a natural sequence that needs to occur. For example, if you had the following three DERs for a set ninety-day period, which ones would you get done first?

- launching your new website
- getting branding work done
- launching your new podcast

These three items may seem to carry the same weight at first glance. But there is a logical order to them if you think about it. If this were my business, the branding work would get done first because there is no point in having a beautiful new website with an old, outdated logo and colors. I would then launch the website followed by the podcast. After all, what is the point of having someone listen to your amazing ideas if you don't have an attractive place to host them?

When you've decided upon your three DERS, you're ready to move on to the next pillar.

### Pillar #3: Saying No

Once you have a clear vision of what you want to make happen in the next ninety days, we need to tackle this big question: *What might get in the way of me accomplishing these tasks?*

In my mini-course "How to Be Productive for Mamapreneurs," I go deep on this topic because we women struggle so much with letting go. We feel that we need to be all things to all people, and we often put our own wants and needs last on the list, usually at the expense of business growth.

But what if you got really good at saying no? How might saying no make an impact on your ability to get important stuff done? How would it affect the results in your business? What if you took your business as seriously as the way you'd approach a full-time job? Chances are it would make a big difference in the long run.

Here are a few questions to ponder that will help you gain the clarity you need:

- **What projects are keeping me from achieving my DER?**
- **What commitments are keeping me from achieving my DER?**
- **What habits are keeping me from achieving my DER?**
- **What opportunities (or "not-portunities" as I call them) are keeping me from achieving my DER?**
- **What relationships are keeping me from achieving my DER?**
- **What competing goals are keeping me from achieving my DER?**

We do this work because I firmly believe if an item on your to-do list is not taking you closer to your goals, it's taking you further away. Too often I see women fritter away their time on tasks that do not move their business forward.

So, now that you know what stuff is getting in the way of you being your most productive self, it's time to rid yourself of the burden. Since

I know we all struggle with saying no, I've prepared this handy-dandy script that will help. It goes like this:

## Not-portunity Rejection Script (or How to Say No, Politely)

*"Thank you so much for thinking about me for this.*
*Unfortunately, due to my schedule, I am not able to commit to this at this time.*
*Thank you for understanding, and I wish you the best."*

This three-part script follows the "shit sandwich" rule I learned from my friend Jamie, who was a grade school teacher for many years. Jamie taught me that any time you need to deliver negative feedback or news, you want to surround that shit with some positive sunshine!

So, sentence 1: *Thank you so much for thinking about me for this* shows the person that you're happy and grateful they considered you.

Sentence 2 of the "shit sandwich" is the shit itself: *Unfortunately, due to my schedule, I am not able to commit to this at this time.* This sentence is the part that could be construed as negative.

Sentence 3: *Thank you for understanding, and I wish you the best.* By wishing them the best, we bring back those positive vibes, ending on a happy note.

Voilà! We let them down easy, and they have no clue they got rejected. Mastering the fine art of saying no to what is not serving us is essential to having a joyful schedule that feels productive.

## Pillar # 4: Resources and Results

There's a trap that I see people fall into time and time again when it comes to their pursuit of "success." I call it the RRC: The Resources vs. Results Conundrum.

To put it simply, we want to achieve ambitious results, but we do not arm ourselves with the right resources to do so. Thus, we don't achieve the results and we get mad at ourselves, thinking it's our fault, that we're not good enough, smart enough, or productive enough to achieve great things.

**Newsflash:** We are smart enough, good enough, and productive enough. It is simply a matter of not having the right resources.

**And guess what? We can always find a way to get or create the right resources.**

Think of it like this: Imagine you go to the grocery store with $100 in your pocket. You fill your cart with what experience has taught you is a load worth about double that amount. You arrive at the checkout and the cashier informs you that your bill comes to $200. You look in your pocket and locate the $100 you placed there just hours ago. You can't complete the transaction, but not because of some fault of your own. It's not as if you're "bad at shopping." You simply didn't bring enough of the right resources to get this particular job done.

You now have two options:
1. Buy less stuff
2. Get more money

The concept is so simple, and yet we do it all the time. We sit down to accomplish a task, hoping with all our might that we've got enough time to get the task done, but in the end, we don't.

This is the Results vs. Resources Conundrum.

So, before you go abandoning all your big goals and dreams because *Lianne told me I don't have enough time*, think about this: You can still accomplish anything you set your mind to, so long as you have the right resources. And those resources are **time, mental energy, and money**.

Looking at your current DER, do you have enough time, mental energy, and/or money to complete this goal?

If the answer is yes, congrats! You're on your way to a blissfully productive state! You champ, you!

If the answer is no, what can you do about it? Do you need to allocate more funds to hiring someone who can help you get over the finish line? Can you carve out more time in your day by simplifying your schedule? Can you throw more energy at the situation by starting this task earlier in the day when you're freshest?

Again, don't be the gal who doesn't bring enough cash to the grocery store. Being a successful business owner requires self-awareness. Accurately assessing how much we are capable of can be hard. But here's a little side tip I'll throw in for fun:

*The more you know yourself, the more success and joy you can create.*

So go ahead and list how much of the three resources you have to hit your ninety-day goal.

**How much money do I have to allocate to my DER?**
**How much time do I have to allocate to my DER?**
**How much mental energy do I have to allocate to my DER?**

Be honest! A lot of us actually have more time than we think we do to complete a goal, but we're just not using that time wisely—something I talk about in the next pillar.

## Pillar #5: Batching and Blocking

When I teach these two concepts, I always teach them in tandem because they really do go hand in hand. Batching is the act of grouping like tasks together. Time Blocking is the act of blocking off chunks of time in your calendar to complete each group of tasks.

When we apply these two significant concepts to our weekly schedule, we find more flow in our days and get more done, which in turn leads to a more joyful business. Instead of feeling like we're swimming upstream or flitting from task to task, we have a focused, streamlined way of approaching our business. We end our days feeling grateful for our ability to complete what we set out to do. We end our weeks feeling confident and knowing we're on track to hitting our DERs. We end our quarter having achieved those DERs and celebrating those wins, then we calmly move onto the next. We end our year being that much closer to our 5YV.

Sounds pretty dreamy, doesn't it? It is, but it's the exact opposite of where I see many women all too often: stressed, panicked, and starved for time.

Now, in order to begin Batching, we must first get clear on a few key things:

## 1. What are all the tasks vying for my attention?

Take a few moments to list out all the tasks you need to complete every day, week, or month. I know you're probably thinking that that's a LOT. But go ahead and make a start on this list. You can come back to it and add to it any time you wish.

Once you have a complete list, what you'll likely see is that your business requires you to wear a lot of different hats. Some of those hats fit perfectly and suit you so well. Some of those hats don't suit you at all. In short, not all tasks are created equal.

## 2. What are the tasks that fall within my Zone of Genius?

Next, I want you to look at your list and put an asterisk beside any tasks that fall into your Zone of Genius—the realm of things that you do really well, that have the most impact on the business, and that have the most likelihood of getting you to your 5YV. Here's a simple diagram that will help illustrate what I'm talking about:

So, looking at your master list of tasks, put an asterisk beside only those items that fall into the center part of this beautiful diagram. Your Zone of Genius is the area where you have met all three of these criteria: 1) You're great at it, 2) You enjoy it, and 3) It makes an impact.

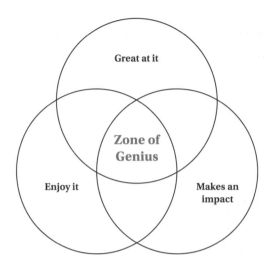

### 3. What are the things that do NOT fall within my Zone of Genius?

Once you have completed this exercise, the items that are not within your Zone of Genius are literally everything else on this list. When I ask women to do this activity, they come up with all kinds of tasks not within their Zone of Genius—tasks that turn out to be bogging them down. This list includes tasks like:

- checking and returning emails
- scheduling calls/appointments
- creating/sending invoices
- booking and managing travel details
- purchasing and sending client gifts
- updating website/contact details
- making payments
- setting up software systems
- tracking and recording metrics
- managing social media

I am extremely intimate with most of these items because I once erroneously tried to do many of these same tasks, back in the day when I didn't believe in having a team. Thankfully, I have since handed off these tasks to someone on my team better suited to handle them.

The next step is to take this list and group these items into categories. For example, creating and sending invoices and chasing payment fall under the same category: business finance. Writing creative copy for emails and creating social media posts and ad campaigns fall under another one: marketing.

See if you can group all your remaining tasks into the following six buckets:

- Content Creation
- Marketing
- Sales
- Servicing clients
- Finance
- Administration/Other

Once you've done this "bucketing" work, you've mastered Batching. Have something on your list that doesn't fall into a bucket? Create a "Miscellaneous" category and place all misfit tasks in there.

So, if you're with me, and you've done this work, it's time to start Time Blocking. Don't worry if you've never done it before or if your current schedule is a disaster. We start by setting some intentions around the kind of schedule we'd like to create and then go about making the necessary changes to implement it.

The key is to design your Dream Schedule first. Have a vision for the kind of weekly schedule that feels the most joyful to you. Here's a template for you to use:

|  | MONDAY | TUESDAY |
|---|---|---|
| 6:00 AM |  |  |
| 7:00 AM |  |  |
| 8:00 AM |  |  |
| 9:00 AM |  |  |
| 10:00 AM |  |  |
| 11:00 AM |  |  |
| 12:00 PM |  |  |
| 1:00 PM |  |  |
| 2:00 PM |  |  |
| 3:00 PM |  |  |
| 4:00 PM |  |  |
| 5:00 PM |  |  |
| 6:00 PM |  |  |
| 7:00 PM |  |  |
| 8:00 PM |  |  |
| 9:00 PM |  |  |
| 10:00 PM |  |  |
| 11:00 PM |  |  |

Using the Time-Blocking Template, there are five types of time we need to block off:

1. "Untouchable Time"     4. CEO Time
2. Booked Commitments     5. Other Priorities
3. DER-Focused Time

| WEDNESDAY | THURSDAY | FRIDAY |
|-----------|----------|--------|
|           |          |        |
|           |          |        |
|           |          |        |
|           |          |        |
|           |          |        |
|           |          |        |
|           |          |        |
|           |          |        |
|           |          |        |
|           |          |        |
|           |          |        |
|           |          |        |
|           |          |        |
|           |          |        |
|           |          |        |
|           |          |        |
|           |          |        |

Each one of these types of time plays a critical role in our happiness, but they're not all created equal. So it's essential we move through them in a specific order that I've mastered in my own time-blocking journey.

## Ready? Let's start blocking!

### 1. "Untouchable Time"

The first thing I want you to do with your blank canvas is to use a pencil or highlighter to block out what I call "Untouchable Time." This is any time that will not be allocated to specific tasks because it is time you have committed to being with yourself or your family. For most of my mamas, this is the period of time when they're with their children, typically breakfast time and getting them ready for school, and evening time including dinner, family time, and bedtime.

If you don't have kids, this may be any time you want to reserve for yourself. Or it may be time that you want to be "off" for everyone else, time that includes things like your own personal morning routine or bedtime ritual. Basically, it's any time you don't want "touched" by anyone or anything else.

Once you've blocked off that time, we can then start to block the rest.

### 2. Booked Commitments

These are the must-do items in your business and typically include the tasks that occur at the same time of week, every week—tasks that must happen *or else*! For me, these tasks are primarily my coaching calls.

Once a client books in for a call, it is pretty much carved in stone.

Because coaching is such a big part of the impact I make in this world and my own personal revenue, I treat those scheduled appointments with the utmost respect and care. So, for me, large blocks of Tuesdays and Wednesdays are devoted to my client work.

What do you do every single week that is a nonnegotiable aspect of your business? Tasks that are consistent and essential to generating revenue? Block that time off now.

Ideally, by this point, you know the importance of grouping like tasks together, so you're not blocking off an hour here and an hour there. Your Booked Commitments should be large chunks of time when you don't do anything else. So, think blocks of two to three hours versus those scattered all over your week.

**A word about client-facing time:** If you have a business where you have frequent contact with clients, dedicate certain days to doing this work and certain days for other tasks. This separation has helped me immensely. For example, I am writing this book right now on a day where I have ZERO calls booked with clients. It is wide open for me to really sink into the task of creating and to feel delighted in the process. If I had to abruptly stop writing because I had a coaching call, I'd be limiting my ability to create my best work, and frankly, I'd be more than a little irritated.

### 3. DER-Focused Time

Here's where you get to block off chunks of time dedicated to achieving your DERs. So again, if your DER is to start a podcast, then perhaps you want to devote three hours per week to doing that work.

Two key principles I think are important here:

1. Energy Management
2. Task Alignment

Energy Management: Make sure you are making time for DER-related tasks when you have the highest amount of one specific resource: mental energy. Tasks that require you to be mentally alert should probably be earlier in the day and possibly earlier in your week.

Task Alignment: Make sure you're not trying to squeeze your DER time into a day when all other tasks use a completely different part of your brain. This type of schedule can create a lot of strain for your mind— maneuvering back and forth between different types of thinking—and can lead to you getting less done.

I mention this suggestion because a DER like "launching a podcast" is highly creative and requires a lot of time and space to get stuff completed. If you have sandwiched your block into a day where all your other tasks are more technical or analytical in nature, you are putting too much stress on your brain. Attempt to keep creative tasks and analytical tasks separate, and you'll find more flow.

### 4. CEO Time

I highly recommend that you block off time at least once a week for what I call "CEO Time." This is your time to think and generate your most powerful ideas. All the top CEOs of the biggest and most successful companies will tell you that their best ideas come when they have mental space. Sara Blakely, founder of Spanx, said she gets her best ideas while in the car. I personally get my best ideas when I'm on a run or swimming. There's something about our minds being completely away from the business and involved in some mundane and perhaps repetitive tasks that allows for our best ideas to flow.

But the problem is that CEO Time doesn't just "happen." We need to make it happen by blocking it off in the calendar. I personally recommend blocking off one to two hours later in the afternoon, at least one to two times a week. Go for a walk around the neighborhood or take a yoga break—whatever you can work into your schedule that allows your mind to wander. Even just a few hours a week of CEO Time can help you develop new ideas for your business. It might feel indulgent, but the truth is that if we're not making time for creative thinking, then how will we ever innovate?

I make time for CEO Time almost daily, and I often post about it on social media, which has inspired many others to do the same. Nothing makes me happier than when I see one of my Instagram followers practicing and celebrating their own #CEOtime.

## 5. Other Priorities

Lastly, once you have blocked off your "Untouchable Time," your Booked Commitments, and time to work on your DER, now it's time to block everything else. What things are important to you that you want to ensure you make time for? These things might include some of your favorite interests or hobbies.

**Is staying in shape important to you?** Great, me too! Block off your workouts right now so you never miss one.

**Is spending time with your partner essential to your happiness?** Block off those weekly date nights ASAP, and book that sitter!

**Want to make time for growing your knowledge?** Perhaps add in a few blocks dedicated to learning and development each week.

If it is important to you, it goes on the Time-Blocking Template. If it's not on there, you're leaving it up to chance whether it happens or not, which tells me it's not really a priority.

Now that you've done this work, you likely feel the bliss that is associated with organizing your most precious resource of all: your time!

This exercise is not meant to sustain you forever, though. This exercise is just the intention-setting portion of our program. The next step is equally (if not more) essential to a joyful schedule.

## Pillar #6: Protecting Your Blocked Time

It goes without saying that it's not enough to just block off time in your calendar. We have to go the extra mile and protect that time like a fierce mama bear protecting her young. If we don't, then all the efforts we have gone through up until this point are a complete waste.

Protecting your time is simple. All you need to do is ensure that no person or thing stands in the way of you using that time for the purpose intended. You must ensure that anyone around you (your family or team members) knows and respects that you are focused on a specific task and that you are not to be disturbed for that period.

It's also helpful to minimize other distractions. For example, as I am typing this chapter, I have closed out all other windows on my computer, most notably my email. I don't need other items popping up on my screen; I have something much more important to do right now.

Here are some other distractions you may need to minimize:
- smartphone notifications for text and email messages
- your phone ringer
- pop-ups on your computer
- other people's voices in your workspace

Heck, when I'm working on an important project, I even put a sign on my front door that says, DO NOT KNOCK OR RING.

It may take a bit of practice, but trust me, protecting your time is one of the most powerful things you can do to ensure that you achieve your big goals and dreams. If it matters to you, make it a true priority and use the time you have dedicated to it as wisely as possible.

## Pillar #7: The Right Tools

When I see someone who struggles with getting stuff done, it's often because they lack the right tools to do so. Now, don't get me wrong. I don't think having a pretty pink planner is going to magically turn you into a time-management master. You need to do the above work first, get clear on what is (and is not) important, manage your resources, and batch and block off your tasks. You need to have a plan for being productive.

But once you have that plan, I recommend investing in a paper planner that helps you map out your priorities every week.

We are visual creatures, and yet so often we rely on a very unreliable tool to help us get stuff done, and that tool is our memory. Many of us walk around all day with no clear plan written down, and we rely on our memory to help us keep track of appointments, goals, and priorities. But our memory simply cannot store all that information.

We need to see our week laid out in front of us in living color.

Invest in a paper planner that can live on your desk in your workspace, so you always know where you have commitments and where you have some white space in between those commitments.

*Why a paper planner, you ask?*

The act of physically putting pen to paper has a more profound effect on us than typing something into our laptop or phone. We are much more likely to retain the information we've just drafted if we write it down, therefore making our plans much more likely to come to fruition.

I also believe in seeing your whole week in one shot, all the time. If your schedule is locked away inside your phone or some other device, you need to first turn on that device, open the program, scroll through it, etc., before viewing your weekly schedule, which is not the same as having it open on your desk all day. Seeing your schedule a day, week, and month at a glance should be easy to do. Electronics make viewing your schedule more challenging, thus creating a roadblock to your own efficiency.

My favorite tool in this department is the *Live with Purpose Planner* by Peter Pauper Press. I have purchased this planner for the last four years, and I love it because it's big (I like a nice big planner so I can write down every detail of my week) and because it is laid out in the way that my brain thinks about time. When you open it up to any given week, each day is a vertical column running down the page with the hours of 6:00 a.m. to 11:00 p.m. clearly mapped out from top to bottom. Each "day" is about two inches wide, giving me ample space to write in all my appointments. Using this planner brings me immense pleasure.

I encourage you to hit up your favorite office supply or stationary store and browse until you find the planner that strikes a chord with you.

The most important thing when it comes to tools is that you find what works for you, and you stick with it! Can't find a tool that suits your exact needs? Make your own or hire a graphic designer to create something for you.

Another favorite tool I use to manage my time is one I created myself. It's a vertical piece of 11" x 20" paper that hangs on my office corkboard. On it I map out the upcoming quarter at a glance. It contains every important event, launch, promotion, or commitment I have for the next three months, all on one page. It serves a different purpose than my paper planner, which is a more detailed look at the week ahead. Rather, this tool gives me that bird's-eye view of what's coming down the pipeline for the next twelve weeks in one quick shot. It keeps me focused and on track.

The right time-tracking tools are not complex. They are simple, easy to access and implement, keep you on track, and help you move forward toward your big vision.

Here's the last thing I will say on scheduling, and it's kind of like what I mentioned earlier. Everyone's looking for the perfect time-management system or tool that will unlock the keys to getting more done. But the answer doesn't lie in the perfect tool. It lies in you. It lies in your intention, no, your *commitment* to achieving your DERs.

**Are you committed to achieving your goals?**

If not, let's start now. Make a commitment to begin doing more of what brings you joy. Commit to what makes a real impact, not to what doesn't. Begin with this commitment in mind, and the rest will fall into place.

When my son, Alex, was born, it was just a few weeks before Christmas. I was new to being a mom of two, and my own memories of Christmas as a child, while joyful, were not perfect. I recall my own amazing mom spending countless hours cleaning, baking, and prepping for parties and carting us around town to this event or that obligation. I realized that I didn't have many memories of my mom having *fun* at the holidays.

I wanted things to be different with my own kids.

I vowed that I would be present with my kids during the holidays, and together we would only say yes to our favorite activities and politely decline all other offers. This vow has meant that I've been left off guest lists to parties and have missed out on neighborhood events, but frankly, I don't care one bit. What matters most is that my family and I get to enjoy time with each other that is free of stress and obligation. If I really looked forward to those events and found them joyful, we'd be there. If I'm ever in doubt about whether or not to hit up a certain function or event, I ask my kids, "Is this important to you?" If it matters to them, I make space for it. But most of the time it doesn't, and we do what we want instead.

Time is our most precious resource. Unlike money, we can't earn more of it, we're never sure when it will run out, and once it's gone, it's gone. Let's make the most of this resource. Reclaim your time and start creating an intentional calendar, one that brings you joy and lights you up every time you see it.

Now that you know how to have a more joyful schedule, and you're prioritizing your big business goals, I also want you to consider how you'll infuse that schedule with a little fun!

CHAPTER 7

# YOUR JOYFUL PLAY

I remember it like it was yesterday. It was a cold, dark day in winter. My husband and I had not been getting along for a while. He had been grumpy with me and the kids and had become short tempered. I was no better. I was snapping at him because I blamed him for my bad mood. I felt deprived of the ability to do the things I loved, and I was taking it out on the children. Rather than looking for opportunities to enjoy life, I was making a list of all the things that were wrong with it and me. That list looked like this:

- I'm not making the money I want to make.
- I have a knee injury that keeps acting up, so I can't go for a run.
- My kid keeps acting out, creating more tension in our house.
- My husband doesn't appreciate me.
- I keep eating like crap.
- I have no energy.
- Someone left a snippy comment on my Facebook post.

The list seemed to go on and on, and if I'm honest, I was intentionally adding to it. Have you ever done this? When things seem bad, you start looking for more proof that it's bad? I mean, talk about self-sabotage.

And then, something happened.

I found out a man I had worked with for many years at a past job had passed away. He had become ill with a rare disease and had deteriorated quickly. Before I had even known he was sick, he was gone, leaving his wife and young daughter behind.

He was thirty-eight. I was forty-two.

In my grief I realized just how flippantly I had been treating my own life—how much I had been taking for granted. Here I was, just a few years older than this man, grunting and groaning at every turn, looking for more misery even though I had a great life. I had my beautiful children and husband, a roof over my head, a career that I loved, amazing friends, and my health. While I was complaining about how hard my life was, my friend would have given everything to live just more days of his. Talk about a reality check.

One of the things I believe keeps us feeling young and vibrant is to include play in our lives.

What is play? It's anything you do 100 percent for fun, and not because it will make you look good or make you smarter or more popular. Play has no side benefits. It exists merely to bring you joy.

For example, when I think of my kids playing with Lego (currently their favorite toy), they're not doing it for a specific reason or outcome. They're not being competitive or trying to challenge themselves. They're just having fun. They can go on and on for hours doing just that one thing.

*What is that for you?*

I know this question can be hard, and it seems to get harder to answer the older we get.

What do you absolutely love to do? Even I have a hard time with this question. When I think of working out, for example, I know a big part of my enjoyment in it is because it makes me look and feel my best. If I could look and feel that way without working out, would I? You bet I would!

Here's a list of the things I love that serve absolutely no other purpose than sheer joy:

- gabbing with my girlfriends over a cocktail on a patio on a warm summer night
- splashing in the waves at a gorgeous beach with my two kiddos
- watching a really good stand-up comic (live or on TV)
- going for a bike ride with my husband to Evergreen Brickworks
- cooking a nice meal for my family
- painting with acrylic paints on canvas (I haven't done it in a while, but I do enjoy it)
- exploring a new area that I've never been to before
- sipping a latte in a cozy cafe while journaling or mapping out next year's business strategy (and yes, this activity IS fun for me)
- watching a musical performed by exceptional artists on stage (my most recent fav was *Come From Away*)
- getting on a plane by myself
- spending a day at the spa
- having "Friday Movie Night" at my house with my kids and a nice bowl of hot, buttered popcorn
- writing this book

I'll be straight with you. While I'd love this book you hold in your hands to hit the *New York Times* bestsellers' list and become an instant success that results in millions of raving fans and oodles of dollars in my bank account, that is absolutely NOT why I'm writing it.

I'm writing this book because it lights me up to do so. The thought that thousands of people will read these words one day and, as a result, make some changes to their life that will bring them more joy, well there's nothing that seems more fulfilling to me than that.

So, just like in previous chapters, I present you with a few questions that will help you make your own list of activities that bring you joy:

- **What thing do you love so much, you smile just thinking about it?**
- **What activity or hobby could you do all day long?**
- **What activity makes you feel more alive than anything else?**
- **What's something that makes you feel relaxed and at peace?**
- **What's something you would miss if you couldn't do it anymore?**

### The harsh reality

Most adults make little time for what brings them joy, and the saddest part is that they neglect to do so under the guise of being "productive." They'll claim they simply don't have time to do "X" because they're too busy running their business, for example. But they started their business so they could have more joy. So, what's up with that?

### Since when did "busy" become the goal?

If we're not prioritizing the things that bring us joy, we end up playing the victim. Our business runs us and not the other way around.

If this situation is happening to you, revisit Chapter 6 on Joyful Scheduling and start making room for the things that light you up. Get those things on your schedule early and often.

I think of my friend Jen who has loved riding horses since she was a little girl. She gave up riding for many years in the name of building her career, but she's recently taken it back up because she missed it and because she never found another activity that made her feel so happy and alive. She now schedules riding into her week, blocking it off as "Untouchable Time," because to her, it's a nonnegotiable appointment with herself. It's a true act of self-care.

Did you know that I typically book my vacations at least one year in advance? This fact is true for family trips, girlfriend getaways, and my annual women's retreat. Once something is booked and paid for, in my mind, it's happening. Nothing will stand in the way of me and that margarita by the pool. I then block off that time in my calendar and let my team know. This blocking allows me to plan around this time, meaning all work engagements must happen either before or after each trip so that I can be fully present for my family (or even just for myself) while enjoying some downtime.

This act also simultaneously primes me for joy. It forces me to "bake the fun" into our annual schedule, and if done well, I experience some sort of magical adventure once a quarter (at the bare minimum).

Here's a look at my annual vacation schedule:

**December:** Two weeks off for family time

**January:** One-week "working holiday" at my women's retreat

**March:** One-week family vacation in someplace warm

**July:** Ten-day family vacation (usually a road trip within Canada/US or Europe)

**September:** Three to five days off with my husband for our anniversary

In addition to this "rigorous" travel schedule, I take several mini breaks per year. For example, I often participate in mastermind programs with their own retreats built in, and I so enjoy these learning vacations. I also layer in some getaways with my gal pals. And last but not least, my husband and I love to get away to the Niagara wine region for a few days each year so we can bike the vineyards and do some tasting along the way.

Notice anything about my vacation schedule? I'm getting away from regular daily life about once a quarter for a least a week. The one exception is in the fall because those months are my busy season, and I've embraced that fact. Come September, all my women are in back-to-business mode. Once they send their little ones back to school, they're extremely motivated to return to their own goals and learning.

It's also the season I host our largest event of the year. Since its inception, our annual conference has taken place at the end of October. It's my favorite time of year for that reason. The energy just moves in the right direction, and time seems to pass quickly. While I could easily take a fall vacation, the truth is that I don't want to. I get into a flow, and I'm eager to stay in that flow because work feels fun and effortless.

But aside from fall, I pretty much have something delicious on the calendar every twelve weeks. How amazing is that? I never have to go longer than three months without some meaningful downtime. And I always make the most of that time and return refreshed and excited to get back to my business.

Even during our two weeks off in December, while it is often a "stay-cation," we spend a lot of time doing fun things as a family. I also use these weeks to do things I enjoy but rarely make time for like cleaning out my closet or reorganizing my office.

## Working on vacations

You might be wondering, *Lianne, do you work on vacation?* My honest answer is, it depends. First and foremost, I always try to uphold whatever commitment I've made to my family. If I have promised them that I won't be on my computer, I stick to that promise. I would say that 90 percent of the time I do not work on vacation.

That said, there are times when I am simply unable to set aside work for weeks on end without checking in. If we are in a busy season or my team has particular needs, I may need to check in once in a while.

The last few times I have traveled with my family, I brought along my laptop but never opened it. I usually end up getting so relaxed on the first few days that I have no desire to open the darn thing, and it stays tucked away in a bag the entire time. It is there as a backup should an emergency arise and I absolutely need to step in, or if I feel inspired and want to plug away at an idea while it's still fresh in my mind.

I don't want you to agonize over this decision. You are the CEO of your own company, which is different from being an employee of someone else's business. You are more invested, and you have worked hard to build up the business you have. If bringing your laptop makes you feel more in control and connected, do it. But my hope for you is that over time, after applying some of the principles you've read about in this book, you'll have the freedom and flexibility to completely unplug. It's like the saying goes, *"Almost everything will work again if you unplug it for a few minutes, including you."*

Here's how you know you're doing this chapter right.

You end your days feeling fulfilled, not drained. You end your weeks feeling proud that you made time for what matters. And you end your year looking back on a life well lived. Your business is a success because you've taken great care of its number one asset—YOU!

**Reading the signs**

I couldn't end this chapter without helping you identify some clues that you might not be making enough time for play:

- You are going to bed exhausted at the end of the day.
- You find you are resentful of your partner because he/she always seems to make time for what they love.
- You are skipping out on fun plans on the weekend because you "have to work."
- Your friends stop inviting you to events because they know you'll just say you're "too busy" (this started happening to me not too long ago, and it was a rude awakening).

- Your loved ones start avoiding you around the house because, well, you're a grump.
- Your clients and team members mention that you don't seem yourself.
- You find yourself mentioning the word "burnout."

## The thing about burnout

Most of us don't realize we are burning out until it has already happened. We hit the wall so hard that we crash and burn, but not before taking others down with us. We are struggling in our life, and we take it out on the people we love. (As much as I hate to admit it, I've been guilty of behaving this way.) We've become obsessed with achieving results, and yet the quality of work we put out has been on a steady decline, so we experience "diminishing returns"—the more we work, the less we accomplish.

*So, how do we avoid it?*

We must learn to notice the warning signs I listed. If you see more than one or two of these situations happening to you, there's a good chance you're headed for burnout, and if you're not careful, you could end up doing the exact opposite of what you intended to do with your business.

When you are burnt out, all your energy then goes to resetting and rehabilitating your own self. For some, it can take weeks or even months to recover from burnout. So, if all your energy is going to recuperating, how will you possibly have energy to serve your Dream Clients and make your mark on the world?

Here's a chilling example. Ever heard of Arianna Huffington? Ya, that Huffington. She burnt out so badly that she passed out while working late one night and woke up with a head injury. It was her literal "wake-up call" that something in her life had to change. If you are in this place right now, I feel you. I have been there before, and it can be debilitating.

But it doesn't have to be that way. Every principle I teach in this book is geared toward helping you create a happy life with sustainable healthy habits. Yes, even the chapters on scheduling and leadership, though they may seem like business topics, are powerful lifestyle tools. After all, when you have a successful business that allows you to live your best life, everyone benefits.

Your clients benefit because they enjoy their interactions with you. The result is happy clients who come back for more and bring their friends (cha-ching!).

Your spouse benefits because your joyful habits rub off on them. You inspire them, in turn, to be their best selves. End results equal more intimacy, connection, and yes, more *sexy time*.

Your kids benefit because they get to spend time with "Fun Mommy" and not a burnt-out, angry "Momzilla." They grow up with the knowledge that it's possible to have a great time being a parent and running your own business. The result? They, too, create meaningful careers that light them up.

Your friends benefit because spending time with you is a blast. There's more fun and laughter, and you inspire them to make positive changes in their own lives. The result is stronger relationships and a true win-win society.

You see, when you prioritize joy and play in your life, you're not shirking your duties or avoiding reality. On the contrary. You are infusing your reality with a double shot of joy. Isn't that the point anyway? You're living life to the fullest, which is exactly what you are meant to do, and you're bringing that life and enthusiasm back to your business where you continue to inspire your customers and team.

And speaking of team, you might be thinking, *Lianne, you keep mentioning team, but it's just me in my business,"* and if that's the case, it's time for that situation to change.

In the next chapter I break down why having a team (even a small one) is so powerful in helping you experience more success, more freedom, and . . . you guessed it, joy.

CHAPTER 8

# YOUR JOYFUL LEADERSHIP

I'll never forget the day I was sitting in a beautiful room outfitted with chandeliers and a stunning reclaimed wood table, staring at my coach for hours on end. It was the first time I had engaged the services of a business coach, and the day was simply magical. In just a few hours, she helped me articulate my vision for the business I was creating, and I felt truly lit up by all her prompts and exercises. And then came the question . . .

"So, we haven't talked about the team yet. How do you envision the role a team will play in your growth?"

*Um, I'm sorry . . . what now? Team? What team?*

This was supposed to be *my* business. Just me. I hadn't envisioned the role a team would play in my growth because I hadn't envisioned a team at all!

I promptly told her that I didn't see myself needing a team. I left my old nine-to-five job, not so I could have the headache of managing people but to have the freedom to do what I want, when I want. A team would just drag me down. I wanted this business to feel light as air, and a team, to me, felt hard and heavy and unnecessary.

She simply smiled, tilted her head and said, "You may change your mind on that one day."

And she was right.

It was just nine short months into my self-employment journey when I realized I needed help on the things I had not anticipated. The back-end, behind-the-scenes tasks that were bogging me down. I was spending— nope, scratch that—I was *wasting* several hours per week on tasks that, while I was doing them, made me feel as if I would rather be anywhere else on earth—tasks such as managing data, creating social media graphics, and making simple updates to my website.

As you know, I'm very aware of my weaknesses. For example, here's a list of things I suck at doing:

- anything to do with technology
- anything to do with reports
- anything to do with statistics
- most highly repetitive tasks
- anything that involves me staring at the back end of a website or a dashboard
- printing, signing, or filing documents
- anything involving a password (can we just start using retinal scans for everything already?!)
- creating or refining systems

I discovered within the first few months of running my business that I detested doing these types of tasks. But I didn't do anything about it until about nine months in.

As I've mentioned, it was at that time that I crossed the six-figure thresh-old. My client roster was full, and I was putting in eight- to nine-hour days, Monday to Friday. At least half that time was devoted to client-facing work. I loved my clients and would do anything for them. I wanted to spend even more time finding new and inventive ways of serving them and others just like them. New leads were coming in daily. I was starting to get speaking requests and was scoring some high caliber coaching clients. Everything was going well—except for the fact that I was running out of hours in the day. Every day.

One task that frequently fell to the wayside when life and business got busy was content creation. At the time, I had a blog that I shared dutifully on social media and my email list. It had been getting great traction, and I thoroughly enjoyed writing on different topics that would help my women attract, convert, and serve more Dream Clients of their own.

But confession time: I was often slapping that blog together, with little or no thought whatsoever, on Wednesday afternoons. I was hurriedly typing, uploading, and scheduling in a flurry, all while the rest of my business ground to a halt. After all, if I wasn't blogging, how would I build this business?!

In short, I started to understand the power of scaling.

Now, the word "scale" may sound scary to you, but all it means is to increase something in size and number. When talking about scaling a business, what that really means is finding a way to serve more people and generate more revenue without adding more resources (your time) to get the job done.

For most of the people who read this book, there are two primary ways to scale:

1. Scaling through one-to-many offers (such as an online course or group-learning program)

2. Scaling with a team (bringing more people on to help serve the mission of the business)

In either case, moving from a 1:1 business model (where you serve one client at a time) to a scaled model requires a shift in thinking, but this is a shift that most female business owners are not willing to make. They find it difficult to let go of the original idea of what their business *was* and replace it with what it is *becoming*, and that's why 90 percent of female-run businesses die within their first five years.

So, when you meet a successful woman who has been running a business for five years or more, give that woman a high five because there's a good chance she's figured out how to scale.

In this chapter I focus on the second method, scaling via a team. This is not to say that the first method (one-to-many offers) isn't a great idea. It is, but it's not right for everyone, and it's not the focus of this book. If you want to learn how to scale your business with many digital courses, check out my online program "Launch Rookies" where I teach you all about how to do exactly that!

For now, stick with me here as I do a deeper dive into the importance of team.

So, as I said, I brought in my first team member around nine months into my business. Her name is Nina, and she is a kind soul and a gifted writer and editor. We spoke about the fact that I was finding it challenging to do all the things and create all the content I needed for my business. I thought that if I could dictate my blogs into my phone and send that audio to her, she could take it and turn it into a cohesive, well-thought-out blog each week.

And it worked!

Nina and I started working together in perfect synchronicity. Every six weeks or so I would send her several drafts, and within a few days, I received a Word document that included the same number of beautifully crafted blogs.

The patience and care Nina took with my words was admirable. Writing the material on my own was something I simply didn't have the bandwidth for, or frankly, interest in. I much preferred to speak my blogs because I am, well, a speaker. That's how my ideas flow best. In fact, another fun fact about me is that when I'm working on a new keynote or presentation, I don't start with a pen and paper or even a blank slide deck. I start by standing alone in my house (usually in my living room), pacing the floor and talking. I simply talk out my ideas until they begin sounding like a presentation and then I start making notes around what came out of my mouth.

See, I told you I know my strengths.

The system Nina and I developed worked extremely well for a year and a half! And it would have kept working if I hadn't decided to replace my weekly blog with a weekly podcast.

I so appreciated Nina's ability to take something arduous—a task that was bogging me down—and turn it into something streamlined and awesome. Her work allowed me to focus on those tasks that actually grew my business.

Incidentally, Nina gave me back about four hours per month. Not a ton of hours, granted, but when you're just starting out and you're working on all of the things in your business, four hours a month is a real gift.

Here are some of the things I was able to redirect those four hours toward:

- focusing on high-level strategy
- building and delivering webinars
- creating video content
- building relationships
- growing my email list
- dreaming big

Nina's skill in attacking my blogs with gusto allowed me to focus on some of the most important tasks in my business.

So, if you've already got a team in your business working like a well-oiled machine, congrats! You may not need this chapter. I do encourage you to read it anyway, however, because you may just find a great tip in here that will help you take your team to the next level.

This chapter is really intended for the woman who, just like I did all those years ago, insists with conviction that she doesn't need a team; the woman who fights tooth and nail for the very limited version of herself and her business she has created. It's for the woman clinging to what she knows, what feels simple and safe, that's actually keeping her small.

**Here's the truth:** If you want to have a successful and a joyful business, you need help.

Now, there are lots of successful one-person businesses. In fact, Elaine Pofeldt, whom I had the pleasure of meeting, wrote a book on exactly this phenomenon called *The Million-Dollar, One-Person Business*. However, even the entrepreneurs she featured in that book have people helping behind the scenes. They just might not be working full time.

Guess what? You don't need to start with a full-time team of hundreds either. So relax and breathe as I walk you through this chapter. Promise me you'll keep an open mind.

### Why we can't do it all

I used to think I was a good "all-rounder," and that I could excel at most things in life. But as I headed toward postsecondary school, I realized that this belief was not the case, and I started to embrace who I really was—limitations and all.

We are each born with a specific set of skills as well as a set of what I call "Unique Gifts."

**Hard Skills:** These are the hard goods we learn along our journey that help us get tasks done. Skills include writing website copy, building a slide deck, designing a product, or creating a Facebook ad campaign. Hard skills are usually the things we learn from a course or an individual.

**Unique Gifts:** These are the special talents we are born with or develop naturally over time. Unique gifts include telling a joke with impeccable comedic timing, motivating a room full of people to want to be their best selves, or holding space for someone as they work through difficult emotions. While these skills can be taught, they are more likely innate gifts that lie within us.

The reason we can't do it all is that we're simply not naturally gifted at everything, and we don't have time to learn every skill set on the planet, nor would we want to. Instead, I encourage you to build your business around your "special sauce" (see Chapter 2) and let others help with the tasks you're not great at doing. Here are a few questions that will help you determine where you may need assistance:

- ⊙ **What specialized skills does my business need that are not in my wheelhouse?**
- ⊙ **What tasks are holding me back from the growth I want to experience?**
- ⊙ **What tasks take my attention away from achieving my DER?**
- ⊙ **What tasks could be completed easily and efficiently by someone else?**

### Why having a team is more joyful than going it alone

The obvious reason why having a team is joyful is exactly what I've been preaching to you this entire book: Letting go of what doesn't light you up allows you to focus on building a business around what brings you JOY.

But there's another reason, and it has to do with *impact*.

When we think back to our mission and the impact we want to make on the world, 99 percent of the people who read this book will have some version of "to help people" as part of that vision. We are naturally drawn to helping others as it gives us an immense sense of purpose and self-worth. When we help others achieve their dreams with our products and services, we reach new levels of personal growth and begin to achieve our own version of success.

You will never go wrong (nor will you mess up your business) when you lead with joy, heart, and the mission to make people's dreams come true.

**Case in point:** The more my own business grows, the more women I help with my programs, communities, events, and now, this book. The more those women grow their businesses and their own revenue, they, in turn, will help and serve more people. It's a powerful ripple effect, and it's pretty damn cool.

One thing I did not anticipate when it comes to a team was the pleasure it would bring me to allow my team members to do meaningful work that energizes them. I never expected how much joy it would bring me to coach and mentor my team, but why not? After all, I knew how much fulfillment I experienced by coaching and mentoring my clients.

The women on my team are smart, funny, passionate, kind, generous souls. They believe in doing great work, helping others, and giving fully and wholeheartedly. When I bring my team together for meetings or social gatherings, it tickles me to see the bonds they have formed with each other and how much fun *they* are having working within my organization.

So, while this side benefit wasn't something I had anticipated, it is something that I truly appreciate and want more of!

Leading your team doesn't have to feel hard and heavy. Leading your team can and should feel joyful, and it will when you follow these basic principles:

### Just start with your first team member

I started building my team with one person who gave me a handful of hours each month, which cost me just a few hundred dollars. At the time it felt like a lot of money, but I quickly realized how much money I was gaining through reclaimed time and energy. I learned that my time and energy are my most precious resources, so why waste them doing things that don't bring me joy? Why not empower both myself and another person to operate in our Zones of Genius, thus making my business and our lives more joyful?

Go back to Chapter 6 and do the Zone of Genius exercise (if you haven't yet done so). To recap, make that list of everything you do in your business and then put an asterisk beside the items that fall within your Zone of Genius. What remains on the list are the items that suck the living joy from you every time you think about them. Put those tasks into groups or "buckets" based on your skill set. For example, blog editing, writing website copy, and crafting social media post captions all require the same skill set: excellent copywriting.

Keep doing this activity until you have several different buckets of tasks. Then, when you're ready, each one of those buckets can be turned into a job description. Pick the group of tasks that takes up the most time and/or energy from you each month. You know, the one that really drains you to even think about. Got it? That's the one you outsource first!

### A word about "outsourcing"

I have never liked the term "outsourcing" because it implies that you are sending the work "out" to be completed by some outside source. Rather, I prefer the term "insourcing," which is the act of bringing someone into your organization to manage the work. I'd rather you think of the people who work on your business as your team and not some random group of contractors you simply dump your grunt work on to manage. There's a marked difference between those two approaches, and it will show up in your company culture.

**Note:** I recommend bringing just one new team member on at a time, especially if you are new to hiring. It takes more time and care than you might think to hire, onboard, and train a person to do things the way you want them done. Hiring one person at a time provides you with the bandwidth to really devote what it takes to ensure this person has a strong start.

Once you're armed with your job description, the next step is to share it on some job sites and, depending on your niche, on certain social media sites that make sense. Get the word out about what you need, and typically, the universe will provide. You'll likely have to interview a few candidates before you find the right one.

My point? You can absolutely start small. It doesn't have to take a lot of your time and attention to find your first hire and hand over the reins. But it will require you to take a few specific steps, which I walk you through in the pages that follow.

**Warning:** It might feel tempting to hand this work over to someone you already have in your network who appears to fit the bill. But I caution you not to make a habit of it. Just because your kid's daycare teacher happens to build websites on the side doesn't mean she should build yours. The number of times I have seen someone hand important tasks over to their best friend, former roommate, or sister-in-law just because it seems easier than going through the process I'm about to share— well, it's more than I can count, and frankly, almost always ends in disaster, hurt feelings, and broken relationships. And you still have to find someone to do the work! Take my word for it: Don't just grab the first person within arm's reach who can do these tasks. Take the time and effort required to write a job description, conduct interviews, and select the right candidate.

### Writing a clear and sexy job description

Writing a job description is more like writing killer marketing copy than anything else. Unfortunately, most of us treat it like a chore, and therefore, hiring *feels* like a chore. Hiring should feel like a dream come true because you are bringing a star player into your business to help you achieve new heights. If you are approaching the writing with a feeling of drudgery and disdain, we gotta shift that energy.

The first place I encourage you to start is by imagining that you have already hired the perfect person for this role. Picture her right now.

- Who is she at her core?
- What does she do better than anyone else on the planet?
- What are her strengths and skills?
- What is her attitude like?

I want you to imagine her so clearly that you can picture what she's wearing and how she engages with you and your team. You should be able to see her sense of style, recognize her very essence and personality, and know what she ate for breakfast this morning. I want you to imagine you both sitting in your office, smiling, laughing, and getting shit done. Picture being in the trenches with her, arm in arm, together working in your own Zones of Genius.

Next, take that visualization and write it all down. Capture all those thoughts ASAP.

## My Dream Employee

Now that you have taken time to get clear on what your dream team member looks like, it's time to manifest her into existence. The first and possibly hardest part is to believe that she's out there.

The biggest mental roadblock I see when it comes to hiring is the belief that "good help is hard to find," or some version of that tale. Are you guilty of this self-fulfilling prophecy? Well, let me ask you this question: How easy is it going to be to find, hire, and onboard your dream team when that's your attitude about it? Not very!

You need to completely shift the way you approach this project. You've sketched out your dream team member, now let's go get her! Consider this: You wouldn't sign up for a course that you didn't believe would teach you the skills you want to acquire. You wouldn't go to the mall for a new iPhone if you didn't already know there was an Apple store there. So why are we putting out a job description with the belief that no one good will apply?

I know I am belaboring this point a bit, but read my lips:

*You MUST believe your dream team member is out there, eagerly anticipating this opportunity.*

Once you have done this mindset work and are anticipating finding this person, it's time to craft a really kick-ass job description. Remember earlier when I said that a great job description reads more like great marketing copy than anything else? That's because you *are* marketing. You're selling this person on what a fantastic opportunity it is to work within your team. And it *is* a fantastic opportunity! Don't think otherwise.

Think about it. What can you offer someone who works with you? I'll kick things off:

- experience in their given field
- a positive, friendly working environment (after all, you're reading this book, so your team is going to be a ton of fun!)
- flexible hours
- mentorship from someone amazing (that's YOU!)
- work-from-home privileges

- opportunities to advance based on performance
- opportunities to learn and grow
- fun outings and team-bonding experiences
- the chance to meet new people (your team, partners, clients, etc.)

See! I bet you're thinking, *Gee, she's right. I CAN offer all those things . . . and more!* Or at least I hope you're thinking that way, since you've made it this far in the book.

Working for you can, and should be, a joyful, enriching opportunity, something that many would be honored to get to experience. So, start acting that way! Treat this job description like your chance to share with the world how amazing your company is, what an incredible leader you are, and what a delightful and growth-oriented experience working for you will be. Come from that place and your job description will be an A+.

## My Five-Part JD Framework

Most people have no clue how to write a job description, so I've included my suggested framework right within this book so you can learn how to do it well. I believe that like most things in business, there is no right or wrong. With that said, I see a lot of job descriptions that focus on the wrong things, and therefore, they attract the wrong candidates.

These are the biggest blunders I see. The job description:
- is too short; it focuses only on core duties to be performed
- is too long; it contains an arduous to-do list with tasks that don't sound fun

- is written in a cold, impersonal tone and reads as harsh or demanding
- focuses too much on your needs and demands versus their gifts and desires
- does not address the attitude or personal traits you want to attract
- doesn't "sell" the experience or benefits of working for the organization
- includes poor grammar/spelling, making you, the business owner, look unprofessional

Now that we've covered what not to do, let's look at the right approach. Writing a great job description doesn't have to be hard. You just have to know the right ingredients to include, so here's my Five-Part Formula for the perfect job description (I'll refer to it as JD from here on out).

## Part 1: Job Title and Opening Tone

Most JDs are dry as day-old toast and don't include any sizzle. The first thing people see when viewing a job description is the title of the job you're hiring for, so you gotta give it some flavor. Back in the day when I was a corporate gal, I recall that a job title was this big, all-powerful thing that carried a lot of weight. Now, in the entrepreneurial world, I hardly ever think about a person's title. When business owners agonize over their own titles, I just don't get it. It seems like such a minor detail, and I know in my bones that no external "label" like a job title could ever define my worth.

That being said, giving someone a snazzy title can have additional benefits. For example, if it matters to the individual being hired that they can put "Director" on their résumé, and it doesn't matter to you (and you don't currently have someone on your team with that exact title), why not give it to them? It costs you nothing, but it makes that person feel amazing about themselves, they'll likely enjoy their role that much more, and they may even take the job that much more seriously! While it is about hiring the best fit for your organization, and quite frankly, the best fit for you and your personality / working style, it's also about empowering your new team member to step into their power and greatness. If a job title helps them do that, helps them show up more powerfully for you and themselves, that's a win-win!

The classic mistake I see is that job descriptions just don't sound sexy enough, so a title is a great place to add some appeal. How can you create a job title that attracts eyeballs and applicants (the kind of applicant you actually want)? If you want someone fun and interesting, the title should be fun and interesting. If you want to attract someone more serious, the title should reflect that too. In any event, don't underestimate the influence a powerful title can have on a job description.

Here are a few examples of title makeovers. The titles on the left are the sad, first drafts, and the titles on the right are the jazzier revised versions:

- Virtual Assistant → Office Integrator
- Marketing Assistant → Digital Marketing Coordinator
- Packaging & Shipping Coordinator → Director of Fulfillment
- Human Resources Manager → Director of Human Capital

In these examples I've assumed that you have no qualms with giving someone a director title, even if they're just starting out with you. Again, the old, antiquated system of people needing to "work up the ladder" to first earn the title of manager, then director, then VP, and so on, could not be more outdated and doesn't really apply to the entrepreneurial world.

If your team contains ten or fewer people, I say give the members whatever title tickles their fancy and allows them to bring their best selves to the job. Once you hire a person, you can open up the conversation in that direction, allowing them to try on and even choose their own title. But for our job description purposes, we need something that inspires and excites potential candidates, and it doesn't hurt if it's a little outside the box (like the previous examples).

As you work on the job description, ask yourself this question: *If I were applying for this job, what title would grab my attention and have me put my best foot forward?* After all, there is a good chance that the team member who used to do this job once upon a time was YOU!

Once you've decided upon your title, you want to draft a few opening sentences that welcome the reader into your world and describe what your organization is all about. Don't rush to list out the duties they'll perform without first giving them a little warm-up. It would be like going on a first date and jumping to the good-night kiss before you've even gone to dinner. You gotta romance them a little first. Woo them with your passion for the work you do and why it would be an incredible opportunity to read through the entire description, then hit the apply button.

Writing about your business is a good time to really let your passion and energy for what you do shine through. You don't need to drone on and on about your core values and your mission statement and every sale you've ever made. But you do want to give them a sense of the vibe they are walking into, if hired. Again, think about how you would want to be perceived if you met the perfect candidate for lunch. You wouldn't want to come across as demanding and curt. Rather, you want them to see you as warm, welcoming, and passionate about what you do.

The more you can establish your vision (see Chapter 1) in the words and tone of your job description, the more likely there will be a love connection. You want the reader to fall in love with your vision and leadership style. Many won't. They'll skim the description, decide it's not worth the effort, and move on. That's okay. Believe me, much like attracting a Dream Client, you only want to attract those who really dig what you're all about, so the first few lines of your JD should do exactly that: attract the right people and repel the wrong ones.

## Part 2: Responsibilities

Once you've caught a potential applicant's attention with your enticing title and warmed them up with a few lines about why your business is awesome, now it's time to explain what you're looking for. I suggest starting with a list of four to eight core tasks that will be the responsibility of this person. I like the heading "responsibilities" because it does two key things: 1) it establishes your authority, and 2) it establishes their accountability. Telling someone "here's a list of your duties" establishes a different tone than "here's a list of things we will hold you responsible for." See the difference?

As you list out the duties, think about the Desired End Result you are looking for with each one. For example:

**Duty:** Updating Blog

**Responsibility:** Weekly blog distribution to more than five channels, ensuring a readership of 5,000/week.

Here's another example:

**Duty:** Social Media Management

**Responsibility:** Responsible for crafting and posting four posts a week, ensuring engagement of [insert the metrics important to you and your organization].

When you list out between four to eight major areas of responsibility, you focus solely on the core tasks for which you are hiring. You don't need to list out everything the person will do. For example, if you want them to do your filing, take out the trash, restock supplies, and open and sort the mail, you might just say something like "General office-space organization" and leave it at that. Again, identifying only major areas of responsibility allows you to focus on the general area of need as opposed to the minutia of every task. The right candidates will read through the lines and decide if that area is something they feel strong in.

Here's something to watch out for. If you include too few responsibilities, you run the risk that the candidate might feel there's not enough for them to do and they'll get bored. If you include too many responsibilities, the candidate might feel overwhelmed and experience Imposter Syndrome. Four to eight areas of responsibility is the sweet spot, in my experience.

The key here is to make these tasks that currently feel mundane and burdensome to *you* sound interesting and, well, joyful. Variety is key. If a candidate feels they will be doing too much grunt work, they won't apply. It is important to include a few areas where they can have a little fun or use their creative abilities.

For example, I've coached a lot of interior design professionals who are in need of hiring a junior designer. Their tendency is to list all the hard skills the applicant must have, such as AutoCad (a design software) experience. But what the junior designer may really enjoy is sourcing throw pillows and building relationships in their industry. Don't hire someone to only do your dirty work. You need to keep it interesting. Again, think about what parts of this job lit you up when you first started out. What did you wish you could do more of? There is a good chance the person you are hiring craves the same variety and creativity.

## Part 3: Nice-to-Haves

This section is a little hard to describe, but it's where you list the things that go "above and beyond" the basic skills and roles you're looking for. It's what the French call the *je ne sais quoi*, the indescribable X-factor-kind-of-stuff you just can't put into words. Except you are going to!

This is where we list things like:
- personality traits
- mindset or attitude
- specific types of experiences (such as experience working in small firms, experience with high-volume situations)

I would keep these to a list of two to four things that would be a bonus if you found them in someone but are not core job requirements. Recall that we are looking to attract just a few of these dream candidates in the end, so this section will attract the right ones and repel the ones that are not a fit.

**Part 4: Compensation** (Read: We're awesome, and you will want to work here)
Here's where you sell the experience of working for you and/or within your team. Remember, you are marketing here, and the product, in this case, is the role you are filling. List out the great aspects about working for you, and don't be shy. It is 100 percent okay to toot your own horn. Keep in mind that many candidates may have no clue about you, your company, or its culture, so you want to boast a little. Tell them what they can expect in the form of compensation (if you feel comfortable), and those nonfinancial, but still important, benefits of the job.

I understand that if you are just starting to build your team, this description might feel challenging, and even a little fake. After all, how can you describe what "working for us" feels like if the only person who has ever worked there is you? Well, here's where you need to think long and hard about the culture you plan to create and the kind of leader you want to be. You will need to use your imagination a bit and think once again about how you want this person to feel.

If you want them to feel excited about this job, give them a reason! Tell them what wonderful benefits await them when they join your team. List out all the ways they will be compensated for a job well done.

For example, I know a ton of peeps who would be enticed by the freedom of flexible hours and work-from-anywhere privileges. I know I personally sought to work in environments where I would be provided with opportunities to learn and grow, plus work with mentors. Can you offer your new hire the opportunity to be mentored by you or access to any learning programs you currently own? Can you give them access to your network of industry professionals or professional tools? And if so, what is the value of that?

**A note on including salary:** There are multiple schools of thought on including salary in a job description, and a lot depends on what you're hiring for and what the norms are in your space. When in doubt, including a salary range means you are only attracting people who are truly interested in the opportunity, but you're leaving yourself a little wiggle room.

## Part 5: Next Steps

Most people like receiving specific instructions, and yet far too often we leave too much up to them and then nothing gets done. You need to clearly explain what the candidate should do if they want to be considered for the role. The typical next step is for them to send a résumé (and/or portfolio of their work) along with a cover letter explaining why they want the job. But don't stop there. You should also inform them about:

- the next steps should they be selected for interviews and/or dates you will be conducting interviews
- the deadline to apply
- any additional documents or tasks you want performed as a part of the initial screening process (remember, the more you give them to do, the fewer applicants you will get)

- a sneaky ask to 1) check for attention to detail, and 2) gauge their personality before you even meet them. Think of it as a prescreen ritual.

A "sneaky ask" is when you ask them to do something as a means of weeding out those who don't read carefully and/or follow instructions. It is an excellent way to determine if the candidate pays attention to detail, which is a basic requirement for many jobs these days. Anyone can *say* they are detail-oriented, but you'll want proof. A common sneaky ask is to ask them to put a specific word or phrase on the subject line of their application email. If you are hiring for a sales coordinator, for example, ask them to write "I love sales!" in the subject line. Any application that comes in without that phrase as the subject line can and should be promptly moved to your trash folder. Think about it: if they can't follow the first task you give them, how are they going to operate on your team?

## Interviewing

There's a lot to know about interviewing, so I'm going to give you a guide for it.

### Narrowing Your Search

As soon as applications start pouring in, it's time to start filtering them down to the people who will best suit your needs. You will need a system for weeding out those who are not worth your time and those who will make it to the interview round. How many people you cut at this stage will depend on how many applications you receive. After all, if you get three applicants, you can't very well weed out all of them. Assuming you receive a decent number of applications, here's who I recommend not bringing in for an interview.

- anyone who does not complete your sneaky ask
- anyone who uses poor grammar/communication
- anyone who misspells your name or the company name
- anyone who fails to include any of the items you ask for in your JD

Again, if they are already falling short of your expectations at this stage, how will they perform once they are hired? My recommendation is to only bring in those folks you are excited to meet and who also seem excited about the opportunity.

## Practice Interviewing

The more people you interview for jobs, the better you will be at it. There is a real art to learning to read people's true nature in a short conversation, so it stands to reason that the more you do it, the better you will be at it. I suggest interviewing at least three candidates for every role you fill.

## Practical Tips

I recommend holding interviews in a short period of time; for example, two back-to-back weekdays. By seeing multiple candidates in a row, you will be able to compare and contrast applicants more easily, thus making your final decision less complicated. That said, most people max out at about four interviews in a day. After four, things start to get blurry.

## Virtual Interviews

In this day and age, there is very little reason why you would need to meet a candidate in person, especially if the nature of the role is virtual. I recommend holding interviews via video meeting. This way you can still get a sense of their manner and personality, but you don't have the added hassle of coordinating people entering and exiting your place of work (in many cases, this location will be your home).

Here are a few things to look out for during the interview process:

- **Passion:** Is this person excited by your mission?
- **Communication:** Does this person communicate clearly and effectively?
- **Honesty:** Does it appear this person is telling the truth?
- **Quick Thinking:** Can this person think on their feet and problem solve?
- **Trustworthiness:** Does this person seem like someone you can trust with your business and customers?
- **Initiative:** Is this person a self-starter who requires minimum supervision?

## Making the Offer

Once you've seen all your candidates, I recommend ranking them in order of best choice to worst. This way if your first choice does not accept your offer, you know precisely who your next choice is and can be prepared to make them the offer. Ranking saves you time and energy.

Get in touch with the winning candidate to share the news. Be prepared to provide details about all the essentials such as salary, hours, start date, etc. You want this person to know exactly what you are offering them, so they can accept, decline, or choose to negotiate.

## Negotiating

If your candidate wants the job but isn't happy with some of the terms, they may choose to negotiate. Here is where you need to be firm on what you are willing to budge on and which items are simply a deal breaker for you. You should have already considered whether you are willing to offer them more hours or a higher salary if they ask for it. Come to this process prepared for every scenario, just in case.

My hope is that through this process of creating your JD, and interviewing, you find yourself a real gem who can start right away. You don't want someone sitting on this decision any longer than they need to. If it is a "yes" on both sides, capitalize on this momentum and get this person up and running right away.

## Start Letting Go

This section of the chapter is all about what it takes when properly onboarding and training a new hire. Most people suck at it. The trouble isn't that we don't have the right systems or documents in place. The trouble is that most of us (especially those who are our own sole employee) have trouble letting go.

But when we bring on team members, the main priority is that they free up our time so we can focus on the tasks that matter most.

### Onboarding and Training: What's the difference?

Onboarding is the process of bringing a new team member into the fold. It includes introducing them to your team, showing them around, setting them up on payroll, etc. It is literally the process of bringing someone "on board." Get it?

Training is different. Training provides a new hire with the tools and skills they need to do their job well. Here's what most people don't fully realize (or at least accept). Training takes *time*. In fact, it takes more time than we typically think.

How long should training take?

That depends on how much you expect of this person and the steepness of their learning curve. A general rule is to offer them ample amounts of time in the first three to four weeks. If they aren't fully trained by that time, then either you're not training very well, or they may not be well suited for the job.

In any event, plan to carve out several hours a week to show them how to do their job. Remember that what seems simple to you may not be simple to others. The tasks you can do in your sleep are the tasks you have been practicing for months (or even years). So don't expect them to get it right away. In some cases they may even be a better fit for another area of your company than the one you hired them for. But you won't know it unless you dedicate a couple of hours each week to mentor and train them.

If it takes someone three to six months to become fully operational in a traditional corporate job, afford your new hires the same grace when they come aboard your company. One of the main reasons why certain team members don't work out is that they weren't provided with enough of the right resources and support to do the job well. Let this explanation be a cautionary tale and prepare to set aside more time than you think is required for training.

What should I focus on first?

I recommend covering the vision and values of the company during the hiring and onboarding process. Those items are essential, and it is ideal for a new hire to know them inside and out before their first day on the job.

Then start by walking them through their top three responsibilities in the first week using my **Five-Step Training Framework**.

**Step 1: Explain the "what" and the "why"**
What is this responsibility and why is it important? How does this task relate to the overall mission of the company? How often will they need to do it, and how long do you expect it will take?

**Step 2: Show them how**
Either you or a qualified person on your team should walk them through the process once. As you do, you'll want to capture how you do it. If you're advanced, you'll already have detailed Standard Operating Procedures (SOPs) and training videos on most tasks your team performs,

but if you're not there yet, there's no better time to start! Do a screen recording as you talk them through each part of the process, then save that video to the "training" section of your team management software.

### Step 3: Ask them to do it

Have them perform the same task at least once with you observing so they can ask questions if they get stumped along the way.

### Step 4: Cut them loose

Give them some space to perform this task on their own for a day or so (or longer depending on the length and importance of the task). Let them know that they can come to you (or someone on your team) if they need help. It is at this stage that you want to remind them where any training materials are saved so they can refer to those materials first before coming to you.

### Step 5: Provide direct feedback, in real time

Ahh, the dreaded "F word": feedback. Why is providing feedback one of the most dreaded tasks we as leaders must do? While receiving feedback is a gift, I believe women are wired to avoid conflict. Somehow, we've been trained to think/feel that if someone tells us we need to improve something, we're a failure in massive proportions. Really, all feedback means is that more guidance is needed.

Providing direct and honest feedback in real time is essential to creating a culture where people know it is okay to mess up. Here's a framework for providing constructive feedback (notice I didn't say "negative" feedback. We don't want to label it good or bad—it just is):

1. Explain what you are seeing: *"Hey, Shelly, I noticed you've been sending out client emails with the heading 'hey you.'"*
2. Remind them what was expected: *"You may recall when we spoke two weeks ago that I asked you to please address each client by name in every email."*
3. Tell them the current expectation: *"My expectation is that you'll make things change now. Please stop using 'hey you' and start each email with 'Dear X' and include their first name."*
4. Create a feedback loop: *"I'll be monitoring your progress on this situation. Let's reconnect in one week to see how it's going."*

Remember in Chapter 3 when we discussed providing direct feedback to your customers in real time? The same concept stands here. If you are hiring smart and focusing on providing constructive feedback along the way, you avoid letting issues fester and worsen, and most importantly, you avoid a harsh sit-down where you need to reprimand someone for poor performance.

There is nothing worse than having a semi-annual review in which you learn that there are dozens of areas you need to improve upon, or else. No one wants that situation. So, don't be *that* boss. While I applaud formal approaches to performance evaluation, it can't be the only means of connecting with your team. Providing feedback in real time will improve performance and trust.

## Inspire Growth

If you want to build a rock-solid team of all-star A-players, then you'll want to foster an environment of growth and learning. After all, how boring would it be if everyone on your team performed their duties to the letter with absolutely no desire to move beyond that skill set?

Inspiring growth doesn't have to be complicated. It can be as simple as asking each team member how they'd like to grow. Where do they see themselves growing both within your company and personally? I like to know what people are excited to learn, both on the personal and professional side of things, because everyone is a whole person. I believe that having a full life outside of our work is important, and I want the people on my team to have a robust social life, a rewarding family life, and hobbies and interests that fulfill them because I care about them, and I want them to have the best life possible. But I also want this life for them because it makes them better team members.

Have you ever worked on a team where someone constantly brought others down? They are usually the naysayers and victims who feel their boss, their team, and the world is out to get them. They never seem to have anything positive to say, and they seem stuck. They don't progress beyond their current position, not because they're not capable but because they have no desire to grow. They focus on their current tasks and complete them as requested, but they offer nothing else.

These people don't go above and beyond. On the contrary, they do the bare minimum and say things like "I don't want to give this company one more ounce of my energy than it deserves." Their world is one of "us" versus "them," and they see themselves as separate from the leaders and high performers in the organization. They're always one minute late to the meeting, and they're the ones standing in the corner rolling their eyes when a team-building activity is taking place. They have no desire to grow whatsoever. In fact, their dreams exist outside of the organization. They fantasize about "one day when I leave this place ... ," and it seems the only fulfillment they get is from their personal life.

Everyone knows someone like this person, either from a past or present work situation. Trust me when I say that you don't want this person on your team. These types of people are toxic and serve no purpose within an inspired organization like yours. Even if you have a small team of three to four people, this kind of individual can infiltrate your company culture and shift the energy of the team very quickly. Growth has no room for negativity or anyone not willing to sit in their muck and rise above and push through it. Protect the energy you have worked hard to cultivate within your organization.

So, the first way to avoid getting anywhere near someone like this type of person is to hire smart (as discussed earlier in this chapter). The next way is to develop a culture that values learning and growth over compliance and complacency.

I don't recommend prescriptive growth—when you as leader decide what must be learned and then force it upon the team. It will result in feelings of obligation and resentment.

What we want to do instead is draw out people's unique gifts and see where they have room to further develop them. Where do they have a growing interest that would serve the company? Is there something you are all working on as a team that you can learn together?

Here are some of the ways I have provided (or plan to provide) my team with learning opportunities:

- attendance at live events or conferences in our field
- participation in offsite meetings where team members get out of their normal work setting to brainstorm and share ideas
- registration in online courses that teach skills my team needs
- gifting of books on topics that are interesting and inspiring

There are numerous ways you can provide your team with valuable learning experiences so they grow their own skills (which they will apply to your business) and view your company as a valued learning environment. Their job is a fun place where they get to learn in new and interesting ways and thus, never want to leave.

Learning doesn't always have to be in the form of external resources like books and courses. Learning can be self-directed and more organic based on what is happening in your company at the time. Some of the most valuable learning experiences I've had include having to solve a problem or needing to pivot quickly. The learning came in the real-life, on-the-job scenarios being thrown at me. There was no manual or course I could take to get me through them.

Therefore, where can you be inspiring growth by getting your team to stretch themselves on the job? What situation or opportunity is just waiting for someone to pounce on it? For example, for well over a year I knew I was doing a poor job managing our social media. I was posting intermittently because I felt I had to, but I was putting little (or no) effort into it and viewed it as a chore. And what was the result? Our social media presence wasn't growing, and our engagement with our fans was shrinking rapidly.

That's when I brought on Kirsten. I knew she wanted to build her own skills in helping female entrepreneurs grow their online presence, so I hired her for a few hours a month, and wow! What a difference! Kirsten not only posted more frequently and with more care and attention, she was also willing to explore new opportunities on social media that hadn't even occurred to me. She brought brilliant ideas to the table and made a concerted effort to engage with our fans on social media, something I had neglected for far too long.

While she had only recently started her business and needed to learn some aspects of the role as she went along, she quickly nailed the "voice" of our community and did a stellar job highlighting the success of our members online, which had a compound effect. It made that featured member feel special and appreciated, and it made other mamapreneurs see themselves in our content. It made them feel as if they themselves were being celebrated because so often they saw themselves in our members' stories.

One word of warning when it comes to on-the-job learning, however. Be careful not to put someone in the awkward position of constantly having to put out fires. That is no fun. I recall in my former sales days when I took on selling tours to Asia and the South Pacific. The company was in start-up mode and did not have strong training protocols or resources. It was an "every-person-for-themself" environment. I thrived in the beginning because I am a self-starter and I love new experiences, but then the problems started . . .

One after the next, the geographical regions I was responsible for selling faced some major problems: earthquakes, nuclear disasters, civil unrest, etc. You name it, if I sold it, it was going down. My teammates joked that I was cursed because every time I took on a new country or region to sell, something terrible would happen there.

I didn't mind the challenge at first because I viewed it as a learning experience. But after a while, it became draining. Rather than fielding inquiries from happy, interested leads and selling amazing experiences around the world (my strengths), my days were spent assisting irate customers, navigating genuine crises, and doling out refunds. Over time, I started waking up anxious and began dreading going into the office. I recall speaking up about it to my superior one day, and she calmly turned to me and said, "I get it, and I'm sorry. But this place isn't for everyone. They expect a lot here. And if it's not for you, there's the door."

I read some advice I will never forget in the book *Good to Great* by Jim Collins. To paraphrase, put your best people on your greatest opportunity, not your biggest problem. The previous story is the perfect example of a company that was undervaluing one of their best people by assigning them to problems rather than opportunities. My talents were being wasted, and it slowly killed the drive and passion I had for that role.

### Your learning as CEO

If you expect your people to crave learning and growth, then you need to lead by example. I once had a boss who told our large sales team that it was important they have full lives outside of work; therefore, she wanted everyone to leave at 5:00 p.m. so they could go enjoy themselves. But she worked long past five. On the one hand, she told us she valued "quality of life," but her actions said otherwise. I slowly lost faith in that person as a leader because her actions simply didn't align with her professed values.

It's the old "Do as I say and not as I do" approach. And we all know that leaders who adopt that mindset never fully gain the trust and respect of their people. I believe if it's important to you, you have to *be* about it more than you *talk* about it. The proof is always in your actions—ensure they match up with your desires. It's hard at first, but choose joy and intention every time, and before you know it, your actions will reflect that too.

If you value learning, show it. Let your team in on new opportunities you're working on and invest in courses, books, and coaching that allow you to reach new heights. Rather than keep this work secret, tell them about it! Let them in on a new approach you're learning from a business book and then buy them all a copy so you can discuss it as a team.

I recently told my team that I think we could be doing a better job with email marketing. I knew with a little education and effort, we could be growing our email list and increasing our open rates and conversions at a much higher rate than we were doing.

So, I invested in a course on the subject, and with the course creator's permission, I shared the contents with my team members who work on this area within my business. But rather than just handing off the course to them, I went through the course content *with* them so we could all learn and grow together. After all, if this knowledge is going to make an impact on the bottom line, they may be the ones to implement this knowledge, but I, as a leader, needed to understand it.

While I believe that the boss should be investing in courses and seminars, the value of on-the-job learning cannot be underestimated. We sometimes get frustrated by fruitless projects, and that frustration turns into resentment and anger. But if we stop to look at the learning in those failures, our experience would be dramatically different.

Some of the most painful situations I have experienced as an entrepreneur have led to my biggest learnings. Here's a list of all the things I learned while experiencing pain or discomfort of some kind:

- the importance of protecting my intellectual property
- how to buy out a business partner
- how to move an in-person conference online
- how to fire a team member
- how to fire a customer
- how to survive public shaming
- how to stand up for myself

This journey of business ownership is not for the faint of heart. It really isn't. If I knew how hard it was going to be at times, well, I won't say I wouldn't have chosen it because I feel I was destined for this life. But I know a lot of people expect it to be easier than it is.

Everyone desires the highlight reel—you know, that laptop lifestyle, the glossy Instagram posts, the followers and freedom that comes with it. But very few understand what it means to truly be relentlessly in pursuit of creating a joyful business and life. And often, it comes with a hefty bill of grit and resilience that results from wading through the trenches and carving your own entrepreneurial path.

I won't sugarcoat it. Running an empire is hard work. You will fall down, you will get up, you will be criticized, you will feel hurt, and you will make massive strides, only to later face massive setbacks. You will make mistakes, sometimes big and public mistakes. But through it all, you will learn.

If you can handle all of it, you will be fine.

## Debriefing

One of my favorite activities to do with my team is to hold a debrief after a launch or big project completion. We sit down and talk about what occurred, and everyone gets a turn to speak. We have a framework that we follow that I am offering to you here with the hope it will help you extract the valuable learning from everything you do.

### What worked?

I like to start with this question because too often we look at the painful and difficult parts of an experience first. We focus too much on the limited criticisms we received and focus too little on the positive feedback. Ask each person on your team to offer up what they believed went well with the project and encourage them to share something different than the last person who spoke. Be sure you've done this work yourself first, so you can compare their insights with yours. I do encourage you to share your thoughts *after* the others on the team have gone as it creates an environment of true collaboration and equity. It also fosters trust and connection.

### What didn't work well?

Here's where we can get a little critical. What didn't go as planned? Where did you fall short of your goals, and most importantly, *why* did that happen? Can you trace it back to a single misstep (or two or three)? Can you identify where you might have done things differently and gotten different results? The point is not to criticize yourself or anyone on the team. The point is to see it as a learning experience. Most projects and launches are tests. We don't know the results before we dive in, and we learn as we go.

### What was learned?

List out all the things you and your team learned along the way. I suggest focusing on these three areas: What did we learn about this process? What did we learn about our customers? What did we learn about ourselves? If you look at it as an experiment where you can examine the results from all angles, you will absolutely grow from it.

### What to change next time?

Here's where you can put on your strategic-thinking caps for a bit and think about what changes you can apply to the next project of this nature that will improve results. For example, if it was a promotion and sales were not where you hoped they would be, what can you do to increase those sales? Do you need to market across more channels? Do you need to make the call to action clearer in your copy? Do you need to bring in some affiliates or partners who can help you expand your reach? If we're not asking, we're not learning. And if we're not learning, we're dying.

I hope by now you can see the value of a company that promotes learning and growth, and not just in the team members you bring on but also within yourself as a leader. Doing so will have profound effects on your team, the people you serve, and the impact you make on the world. Leaders go first. Lead yourself and others will emulate and follow you. Remember to allow yourself to be led by others as well.

**And let's face it, it's just more FUN!**

CHAPTER 9

# FINAL (JOYFUL) THOUGHTS

Well, friend, my hope is that by now you are feeling pretty darn inspired to go start or grow that badass business of yours. And I hope you feel that you have a few powerful tools in your tool kit as a result of reading this book.

I want to share some final thoughts with you that will make your journey even more joyful. These thoughts are things I wish someone had told me years ago—they would have made the journey that much more delicious.

You've probably already figured out this fact by now, but my path was not some glossy, pastel-colored road with rainbow sprinkles on top. Far from it! I'm sure you recall several stories in this book describing how I fell flat on my face, and that's intentional. I really want you to see that no one has it all together, all of the time.

## Implementation

I have shared a lot of nuggets of wisdom within these pages, and my hope is that you have had a few aha moments along the way. If you have, I'm truly grateful.

But this book isn't about learning, it's really about *doing*!

Now that we've come this far, I don't want you to simply put this book up on a shelf somewhere to collect dust. No, my friend, for this book to be truly valuable, it's time to start putting what you've learned here into practice.

A great first step is to go back and complete all the exercises. I know that we made an agreement that you would take the time to do them as we went along, but I also know that that is not always possible. Flip back through the pages of this book and revisit the questions and your answers on the downloadable PDFs found at **liannekim.com/bonus**. See what areas need more fleshing out. Where are there a few blanks that need filling in?

Remember, this book is designed to be your blueprint to a more joyful business and life. It's the "plan" you have been waiting for, but you need to do your part.

### Next Steps

Once you have completed the exercises, it's time to start putting steps into practice. But if we're not careful, you may feel like everything we examined in this book has to be implemented all at once, which will land us smack in the center of Overwhelm City! That's not a destination I want you to spend any time in, if I can help it. Therefore . . .

I want you to pick an area of focus for now. Ask yourself this question:

- **What's the one area that, if I started to focus on it, would make the rest of my business feel lighter and more joyful?**

Seriously pause and ask yourself that question. Read it out loud a few times if it helps. You may want to flip back through the different chapters to see what sticks out as needing your immediate attention.

Not making any money? Maybe we need to start generating more leads and sales.

Feeling like you can't play in your Zone of Genius enough? Maybe it is time to hire that first assistant.

Tired of getting to the end of each day wondering where the time went and feeling as if there is nothing to show for it? Perhaps we have to revisit Time Blocking.

Building a joyful, profitable business that fulfills you is something that takes time. Don't expect things to fall into place overnight. They won't. But the great news for you is that even by attacking one of these problem areas with gusto will result in you starting to feel more productive and more joyful. Once you get a taste of that feeling, trust me, you will want more.

In fact, you may decide to tackle one new area of improvement per month. You may wish to start with your schedule because it will have a dramatic effect on getting all other tasks done. So perhaps your DER this month is Batching and Time Blocking until you have the ideal work schedule. Then next month your DER could be to hire an assistant and get them trained so the following month you can set your sights on other DERs.

Start with the tasks that will have the biggest impact on your bliss. These tasks are usually the ones that have been weighing on you the heaviest or the ones that will help you create more time and therefore, freedom.

In my work I come across what I call "Serial Learners"—those people who always seem to be reading a book or taking a course but never apply what they are learning. In actuality, it is a form of "hiding" and playing small because they think if they just enroll in another program that they are doing something productive. But nothing is more productive than putting practices and systems into place that will allow you to truly grow. We must take what we have learned and do something with it! We must take what I call "intentional action." But here's the hard part: I can't tell you what to do. You need to figure that out for yourself.

Think about that joyful business you've been craving, find what needs to shift in order to get there, then take that first step.

### The Role of Failure

I didn't get to where I am today by taking all the right steps, all the time. I got here through taking messy and imperfect action, being open to failing, and picking myself back up and trying again.

But I didn't start out this way. As a "Recovering Perfectionist," I used to have a very strained relationship with failure. I used to think that I was supposed to make all the right moves, and that those moves would always work out perfectly, leading me directly to my Desired End Result. I used to think that successful people were smart, knew all the right things to do and say, and didn't fail, which is exactly why any time I tried something new, I wanted to have the blueprint—the manual to getting it right. I would pay to work with this expert or that pro to hand deliver all the steps right to me, gift wrapped with a bow on top. I figured if I could just get the "right" steps and have a plan, I would quickly and painlessly reach my DERs.

I was wrong. I soon realized that we learn what to do by *doing*. By taking action. Curious, imperfect action. There is no manual or shortcut anyone can give us that will save us from failing.

Embracing failure is especially essential with your marketing strategies. People always want to know what is going to "work" in order to get their audience to know, like, and trust them quickly so they will buy. But the truth is that the only way to know what works is to try a variety of different tactics and see what resonates with your people. I have shared here the concepts that work for me, but what precise message will work on which platform for your unique audience, well, that is going to come as a result of trial and error.

Even to this day, this far along in my business, I may only have a sense of what I *think* will work for my people, but I don't *know* it works until I actually put it out there.

Failure can be your worst enemy if you resist it. But it can also be your best friend if you welcome it with a smile and open arms. It's the best teacher I know, and it is a big part of what is going to get you to that successful, profitable, joyful business you crave.

## Tough Times

I have purposely kept this book positive and uplifting while giving you the proactive approach to growing your movement. My hope for you is that the majority of your days are filled with delightful wins, happy customers, and an overwhelming sense of accomplishment.

That said, there will be dark days. There will be mornings you don't want to get out of bed. There will be times of uncertainty, fear, and doubt. There will be moments when you wish you had a nice cushy day job with a reliable salary (and as much as I hate to admit it, I have had these moments too).

Tough times will come, and when they do, know there is nothing wrong with you. Repeat: THERE IS NOTHING WRONG WITH YOU. Feeling doubt, frustration, and pain is all part of the journey. It's neither good nor bad, it just is.

Perhaps, like me, you might face the sudden illness of a parent. You'll likely deal with stress and anxiety at some point. Some of my clients have gone through painful divorces while coaching with me, and members of my community have endured the excruciating pain of losing a spouse or a child while trying to grow their business. My heart aches for these women.

Or perhaps you will suffer a loss in the business such as the end of a business partnership or the loss of an important client. You may have financial setbacks, a painful legal battle, a public failure, a fall from grace. It's not easy for me to think about it, much less write about it, but each one of these situations is something that I have endured in my entrepreneurial journey.

Know that each hardship is there to teach you something, and the sooner you can look for and find the lesson within it, the sooner growth will happen. In fact, some of my biggest business wins have come on the heels of my biggest flops.

Give yourself a little grace and the permission to feel hurt or down. Know that you are human, and that you are allowed to have bad days. But know that having a bad day doesn't make you a bad person. See each bad day as an opportunity to grow. While my hope for you is that your journey on this planet will be filled with more good days than bad, know that whatever kind of day it is, I'm still here, cheering you on because you are a badass and you got this, friend.

## Courage vs. Confidence

When I ask, "How do you want to feel?," a lot of women respond with some version of "I want to feel more confident." But confidence is over-rated. Confidence is merely the feeling you get when you know you can do something well. For example, as you flip through these pages, you can trust that you are confident in your reading skills. Anyone who has ever mastered riding a bike can say they are a confident cyclist.

So, if confidence is only a result of having mastered something, why are we in such a rush to have it? Shouldn't we be enjoying the journey rather than madly hurdling ourselves toward the finish line? I sure think so.

Rather than confidence, my wish for you is to experience more courage. Courage is a highly underrated state. And it's more than just a state—it's a way of living. Most people aren't born with courage, it's something we develop over time. It comes from knowing that no matter what happens, you will be okay.

If you can cultivate courage, even just a little bit every single day, it will serve you well. You have already demonstrated courage just by picking up this book. By the mere fact that you have started a business or are thinking about starting one, you are illustrating a level of courage that most people don't ever achieve. I didn't have this kind of courage until almost my fourth decade on this earth!

When we show up to an event where we don't know anyone, that's courage.

When we share that first blog post, that's courage.

When we post a video of ourselves speaking from the heart, that's courage.

When we create our first offer and make our first sale, that's courage.

Before there is confidence, there must be courage. Confidence is only there in the good times—it's a fair-weather friend—but courage, on the other hand, courage is there with you in the trenches; it holds your hand while you cry. Courage is what gets you back up on your feet after someone has knocked you down. Courage is that little voice inside you stating, "we got this," even when all your loved ones are telling you it's impossible. **Confidence is the trophy at the finish line, but courage is taking that first step of the race.**

May you have courage, and may you also have . . .

## Tenacity

When I was in elementary school, my teacher wrote a comment about me on my report card. She used a word that I had never seen before. A word that I will never forget.

Tenacious.

Being unfamiliar with it, I thought it was one of those words that sounded fancy and important but had negative connotations like "precocious" or "incorrigible." So I asked my mom about it, and she told me that it meant "stick-to-it-iveness." I liked that! I chose to embrace my tenacity and have worn it like a badge of honor ever since.

Look, I'll be straight with you. I'm not the smartest gal or the quickest (in fact, I often say I'm late to the party on most things). I'm not the savviest or the most sophisticated, not by a long shot. The truth is, I'm not special in any way, except for one . . .

I simply don't quit.

Long after people have told me something is a dumb idea that's never going to work, long after others have given up, I keep going. That's not to say I don't get knocked down; I do. And it's not to say I haven't lost my way a few times. But I always find my way back.

Remember that Five-Year Vision of mine I shared in Chapter 1? Well, I am a long way from that, and I mean a looooong way. Think from here to the moon and back. But that doesn't stop me. I know it will happen, and I hold that vision in my heart, especially on those down days we talked about. I remember that this vision isn't about me—it's about the hundreds, then the thousands, then the soon-to-be millions of people I will help.

You will fall down on this journey. But just as easily as you fall down, you can choose to get back up.

There are countless stories of humble servants who eventually became icons as a result of their ability to stick to the plan. Henry Ford's attempts failed for years before he finally landed on the Model T (*ahem*, notice that no one ever talks about Models A through S?). Thomas Edison is reported to have taken more than a thousand stabs at the lightbulb before succeeding. Much like failure must be a part of your journey, so must tenacity.

Every time you take that next step, even if you're not sure it's the right one, you develop your own stick-to-it-iveness, and that sheer act of just showing up, day in and day out, that's what it's all about.

**Here's the truth:** If running a business were easy, everyone would be doing it! If it were easy to earn a great living doing something you love, with amazing people by your side, well, then, I probably wouldn't have a job—no one would need a business coach!

This path that you're on, it's not an easy one, my friend. But you already know that. This path is fraught with failure, tough times, self-doubt, painful moments—sometimes it's more than we feel we can handle. Trust me, I have been there.

But this path is also filled with beautiful moments of unexpected victory. It's filled with kind and grateful people whose lives you are changing with your work. This path is one of personal growth, and with each step, you are one step closer to your best self. If you take what you learned here with me and you practice it, you iterate, you keep showing up for yourself and for the people who need you . . . if you do all that, there is truly nothing better.

I wrote this book for you, not with the aim of you achieving perfection, but with the goal of you experiencing more joy. Remember this truth as you go and apply these teachings. It's not about getting it "right," it's about having more fun and fulfillment along the way.

Trust that no matter what happens, you will find your way.

# Acknowledgements

This book was made possible because I am lucky enough to have an outstanding team of people supporting me.

First, I want to thank YOU, the reader. Just by picking up a copy of this book, you are helping me fulfill my life's mission, which is pretty damn awesome. Thank you for helping me bring more joy into the world.

Next, I wish to thank my husband, Yoon, and our amazing children for standing by me and cheering me on through this process. You are my light and my reason for doing everything I do.

I have immense gratitude for my talented publishing team who worked tirelessly through many edits and revisions of this book. Tania, Christine, Doris, and Sabrina, thank you for your patience, kindness, and positivity. You rock!

I am forever grateful for my amazing squad of friends who have my back no matter what and celebrate my wins as if they were their own, most notably the milfs and the five crowns crew.

To my business besties: Lea, Cindy, Trish, Amy, and Ashley, thank you for being my guiding light through the tough times and for pushing me when I need it. You just get me, and I am thankful.

To my world-class coaches and mentors: Rick, Shelagh, Ron, Julie, Tarzan, James, Amy, Stu, Jill and Josh, I would not be where I am today without your insight and guidance.

To my clients, members, and students who have trusted me over the years with their big goals and dreams, this book exists because of you. Thank you for allowing me the immense honor of being your guide.

To my incredible team: Camilla, Nicole, Emily, Cora-Lynn, Kirsten, Lyndsay, Anne, Janine, and the other powerhouse humans who have helped further this mission, I am beyond grateful to have the pleasure of working alongside you.

Lastly, I want to thank my siblings, James and Lauren, and my parents, Ron and Carol. I would not be the woman I am today without you. Thank you.

# WHAT'S NEXT?

Well, friend,

I'm hopeful this book gives you the foundation to start and grow an amazing business filled with passion and joy. If you are ready to take that next step, here are three ways we can continue the journey:

## MY PODCAST!

Every week I share my best nugget of wisdom and inspiration on my podcast, *The Business of Thinking Big*. You can find it on iTunes, Spotify, the Apple Podcast App, and anywhere you listen to podcasts, or visit my website: **www.liannekim.com/blog**

## MY COMMUNITY!

Are you a mom with a business or plans to start one? Then we want to welcome you into my incredible community of mom bosses . . . Mamas & Co. Simply visit **www.mamasandco.com** to find out more!

## COACH WITH ME!

I work with a select few entrepreneurs each year to help them achieve their wildest dreams. If you are interested in business coaching, reach out to me at **info@liannekim.com** to see if we are a fit and to book a discovery call.

Thanks, and I hope to connect again soon!

YGTMama Media Co. is a blended boutique publishing house for mission-driven humans. We help seasoned and emerging authors "birth their brain babies" through a supportive and collaborative approach. Specializing in narrative nonfiction and adult and children's empowerment books, we believe that words can change the world, and we intend to do so one book at a time.

🌐 www.ygtmama.com/publishing

📷 @ygtmama.media.co

f @ygtmama.media.co